BIRDS OF PREY

BIRDS OF PREY

Gareth Parry and Rory Putman

SIMON AND SCHUSTER · NEW YORK

Created, designed and produced by
Trewin Copplestone Publishing Limited, London

© Trewin Copplestone Publishing Limited, 1979

Published in the United States by Simon and Schuster
A Division of Gulf & Western Corporation
Simon & Schuster Building
Rockefeller Center
1230 Avenue of the Americas
New York, New York 10020

Library of Congress Cataloging in Publication Data
Parry, Gareth.
    Birds of prey.
      1. Birds of prey. I. Putman, Rory, joint author. II. Title.
QL696.F3P37   598.9′1   79–13544
ISBN 0–671–25151–1

British edition first published as *The Country
Life Book of Birds of Prey* by Country Life Books, 1979

Phototypesetting and monochrome reproduction
by Tradespools Limited, Frome, Somerset
Printed in Italy by
Officine Grafiche Arnoldo Mondadori, Verona

Contents

Page 7   Artist's Foreword
9   Introduction
28   Habitat and Distribution

45	**The Plates**		**Eagles, Hawks and Falcons**	
46	*Plate No.*	*1*	Red Kite	*Milvus milvus*
48		2	Black Kite	*Milvus migrans*
50		3	Swallow-tailed Kite	*Elanoides forficatus*
52		4	Honey Buzzard	*Pernis apivorus*
54		5	Osprey	*Pandion haliaetus*
56		6	White-tailed Sea Eagle	*Haliaeetus albicilla*
58		7	Bald Eagle	*Haliaeetus leucocephalus*
60		8	Golden Eagle	*Aquila chrysaetos*
62		9	Common Buzzard	*Buteo buteo*
64		10	Rough-legged Buzzard	*Buteo lagopus*
66		11	Broad-winged Hawk	*Buteo platypterus*
68		12	Red-tailed Hawk	*Buteo jamaicensis*
70		13	Goshawk	*Accipiter gentilis*
72		14	European Sparrowhawk	*Accipiter nisus*
74		15	Sharp-shinned Hawk	*Accipter striatus*
76		16	Hen Harrier/Marsh Hawk	*Circus cyaneus*
78		17	Montagu's Harrier	*Circus pygargus*
80		18	Marsh Harrier	*Circus aeruginosus*
82		19	Gyrfalcon	*Falco rusticolus*
84		20	Duck Hawk Peregrine Falcon (GB)	*Falco peregrinus*
86		21	Hobby	*Falco subbuteo*
88		22	Pigeon Hawk Merlin (GB)	*Falco columbarius*
90		23	Common Kestrel	*Falco tinnunculus*
92		24	Lesser Kestrel	*Falco naumanni*
94		25	Red-footed Falcon	*Falco vespertinus*
97	**The Plates**		**Owls**	
100		26	Barn Owl	*Tyto alba*
102		27	Tawny Owl	*Strix aluco*
104		28	Long-eared Owl	*Asio otus*
106		29	Short-eared Owl	*Asio flammeus*
108		30	Little Owl	*Athene noctua*
110		31	Eagle Owl	*Bubo bubo*
112		32	Snowy Owl	*Nyctea scandiaca*
114		33	Scops Owl	*Otus scops*
116		34	Boreal Owl Tengmalm's Owl (GB)	*Aegolius funereus*
118		35	Hawk Owl	*Surnia ulula*

120   Acknowledgements

The Common Kestrel.

Artist's Foreword

I think that I began to draw before I can even remember. My parents say that I started scribbling as soon as I could hold a pencil. At first it was military subjects – riflemen, archers and the battle-axe types. Then I went on to trains, cars and motorbikes. One day my parents bought me a book on British birds illustrated by Thorburn and it was from that moment that my interest in birds developed. I joined the Young Ornithologists Club and spent most of my time watching birds and sketching them.

I have always lived in Ffestiniog. The village is perched on a hill overlooking the beautiful Vale of Ffestiniog. I have walked over almost every inch of the district from estuary to farmland and from moorland to mountain.

Together with a schoolfriend (who is now a taxidermist) I was helped and encouraged a great deal by a local schoolmaster, Mr E. V. Breeze Jones, one of Wales's foremost ornithologists, well known in England for his photography and in Wales for his radio and television talks and his books on wild life in the Welsh language. Since meeting him, wild life in general and birds in particular have been my life too.

After school, it was suggested that I should go to an art college, but that was a complete waste of time. I was asked to "express myself" but didn't really know what they meant me to do. So I left after a few months and took a job in the local slate quarry, painting in the evenings.

Mr Breeze Jones took some of my paintings to a small gallery in Bangor – the David Windsor Gallery. The late David Windsor arranged an exhibition of my work and oddly enough all the paintings and sketches – about thirty-two of them – were sold during the private view on the Monday evening before the exhibition was officially opened. There, one of my small, unfinished sketches, drawn in pencil and painted with colours from a child's box, was bought by a Welsh lady living in the south of England. This sketch was seen by someone associated with Trewin Copplestone Publishing who made enquiries as to its origin – it all started from there. Trewin Copplestone commissioned me to paint thirty-five birds of prey for a book and I have been working on these for the past four years.

Each painting takes me at least three weeks, sometimes longer. Most of the birds can be seen locally, so I feel that I know them very well. For the others, I went up to Scotland so as to observe them all from life.

The background to the subject is very important to me. Each painting has to tell a story and the background is a vital part of that story – time of year, habitat, the prey and feeding habits and the light which can affect the colours. It is said that British bird painters tend to over-emphasise the plumage, but at the distance at which the subject is seen in my paintings, the plumage *can* be seen in all its detail. Of course when the subject is in the background the plumage does not show up so clearly.

Nowadays I do sketch a little, mainly rough line studies of birds in flight and in various attitudes. I tend to bring old branches, rocks and rusty barbed wire into the house. But for some reason I have the capacity to memorise things very accurately. After a lapse of a month or more I can still recall details vividly and bring them out of store when needed. And yet I have difficulty in remembering the days of the week!

I am married and have two little daughters, Nia and Llinos. I am Welsh speaking. It is the language of the home and English, in fact, very much a second language. I shall be twenty-eight next month.

Gareth Parry
Ffestiniog, December, 1978

Introduction

Birds of prey, the owls, hawks, eagles and falcons, are the proud freebooters of the animal world – sudden death striking silently and unexpectedly, quite literally as a bolt from the blue; winged executioners, efficient and impassive. This dispassionate mastery over life and death, this easy mastery of the air, together with a certain remoteness, has given them a terrible fascination, rooted in both respect and fear. Generations of artists and poets have felt less an inspiration than a compulsion to try to capture the spirit of these raptors; even the common man has felt their power and weaves them into his superstition and myth.

Biologically, the birds of prey are a diverse assemblage of species which have at different times turned to a predatory way of life. (Although many of the species are referred to as 'hawks' in common parlance, this term should really be reserved for one specific order, *Accipiter*. Throughout the rest of the text, the word hawk is used in this more restricted sense except where it occurs in common names.) The requirements of a predatory life-style are strict and constant; thus natural selection has drawn the same adaptations from all the raptors and all show many similarities in structure and general biology. Most strikingly, all the birds of prey have powerful, forward-pointing eyes. In all other birds, the eyes are set one on either side of the head; this gives good all-round vision but it means that there is only a very small region where the visual fields of the separate eyes overlap, to allow stereoscopic vision. The accurate determination of distances requires the use of two eyes – and to a predator, who needs a highly-developed faculty of judging distances exactly and precisely, this narrow field of stereoscopic sight is insufficient. Thus the eyes have moved forwards in evolution until today they are set together towards the front of the head; the overlap of the visual fields is almost complete. (With the eyes directed forwards, all-round vision is greatly impaired. As a result, a raptor wishing to

Wood engraving of a Golden Eagle by Thomas Bewick from his History of British Birds, *published in two volumes in 1797 and 1804.*

look around must move the whole head to and fro. This facility is most highly developed in the owls, in some species of which the head can be rotated round upon the neck almost in a complete circle – in fact in an arc of some 270 degrees.) Raptors' eyes are large and powerful: the eyes of a Duck Hawk weigh approximately an ounce each – larger and heavier than human eyes. It has been calculated that if our eyes were in the same proportion to our bodies as the Duck Hawk's, a 170-pound man would have eyes three inches across and weighing four pounds each! Further, the whole retina – the layer of light-receptive cells within the eyes – records distant objects with a resolution twice as acute as that of the human eye; where binocular vision focuses, there is a region of close-packed cells which record a resolution eight times as great as ours.

All diurnal birds of prey have this extraordinarily keen eyesight. The owls, by contrast, generally nocturnal creatures which hunt to a large extent by sound rather than by sight, have evolved a different sensory adaptation: powerful ears, set in a dished saucer (the 'facial disc') which focuses and intensifies the sounds. The ears are asymmetrical, too, so that the difference in the sound reaching the separate ears is exaggerated, enabling the bird better to pinpoint direction and distance.

There are other common adaptations to the predatory way of life. All raptors have powerful, hooked beaks for gripping and tearing at their prey. All have heavy, strong feet and claws – talons that may be used not only to catch the prey or hold it whilst feeding, but actually for killing. Many birds of prey crush their victims in their powerful feet. The falcons, which take their prey in the air, have an especially

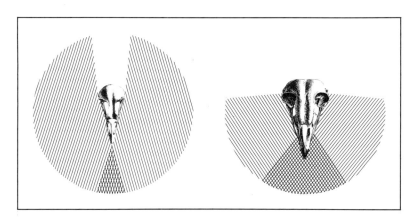

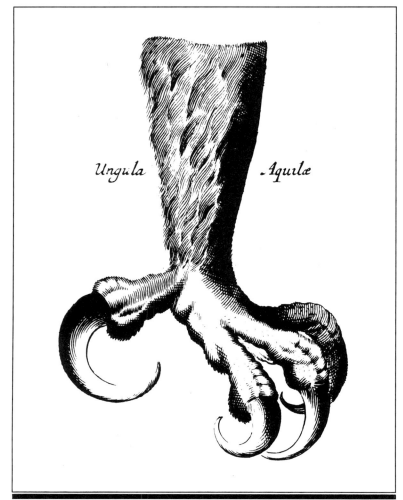

Top: drawings to show the different visual fields of a bird like a thrush whose eyes are at the side of the head (left) and that of a raptor whose eyes are positioned more towards the front. Where the visual fields of the separate eyes overlap is the region of binocular, stereoscopic vision. The area of no vision behind the head is left clear in the diagram.
Above: detail of an eagle's foot from H. Ruysch's Theatrum Universale Omnium Animalium, *published in Amsterdam in 1718.*

long hind toe – the killing toe – which can be used separately to strike their quarry to the ground. Many raptors pluck their prey before eating and, in feeding, strip morsels off the bones with their sharp, hooked beaks. The larger hawks, eagles and buzzards, and the owls may swallow their prey whole. Characteristically, such birds form a pellet of the indigestible portions of their food, such as large bones, skulls, fragments of fur and feathers, and void this later through the beak. Such pellets, often cast below a limited number of favoured roosting sites, can offer a great deal of interesting information on what the animal has been eating.

The general body shape, the pitch of wings and tail all serve their function in adapting the predator to its way of life, although here there is more variability, since the birds differ greatly in their flight and method of hunting. Buzzards and eagles have huge, broad wings, relatively short necks and tails – adapted to high soaring on air currents and thermals. The owls, for their part, have rounded, moth-like wings; the special structure of the feathers on the leading edge of the wings damps all noise so that the flight is absolutely silent. The hawks and falcons offer a splendid example of how different hunting styles impose different requirements for flight. Falcons are typically 'pursuers', chasing potential prey in direct pursuit, or 'stooping' on it from above. There is no attempt at subterfuge or concealment; the falcons rely on speed alone to take their prey. As a result they are slim birds with relatively short tails but long, narrow, sharply-angled wings. The 'true' hawks on the other hand are 'pouncers', capable of extremely high speeds over short distances, but not in sustained pursuit; they are birds of close cover, relying on surprising their prey and closing with it in a short dash. For manoeuvrability in dense cover, (woodland or hedgerow), they have long tails and relatively short, broad wings. They have a far greater ability to twist and turn suddenly in flight than any falcon; one source records a Sparrowhawk flicking through the rails of a five-barred gate intent on pursuit of its prey.

Perhaps the most striking uniformity amongst all the various birds of prey is found in consideration of their breeding biology. All predators – and birds of prey are no exception – operate at the top of a 'food-chain'. There is in the natural world a pyramid of the numbers of organisms, such that there are fewer carnivores than herbivores, fewer herbivores than plants – in terms both of numbers and biomass. This is because each organism requires more of the level below to sustain it – a Sparrowhawk will kill many sparrows during its lifetime and each sparrow will have eaten a great deal of grain. So, numbers diminish up a food chain, and, as a result, for the predator at the top, food is relatively scarce and usually widely scattered. To protect an adequate food supply for breeding, most birds of prey maintain a large territory around their nest site. But even this cannot guard against the unpredictable and irregular fluctuations of prey abundance. Thus the clutchsize or broodsize is adjusted as the season progresses, so that at any time it is exactly that which can best be supported by available food supplies. Such a mechanism has been developed independently in almost all the raptors. In practice, the number of eggs laid depends to a large extent on the availability of food. Further, whereas in other birds the start of incubation is delayed until all the eggs are laid and the clutch is complete, in raptors incubation begins, generally speaking, as soon as the first egg has been laid. Other eggs may be laid – at intervals of one or two days – but incubation is not interrupted. Since the incubation time is the same for each egg, this results in an asynchronous hatching, with chicks emerging at one or two day intervals as the eggs were laid. Thus any nest will ultimately contain a series of chicks of different ages. If prey becomes scarce, the young compete for what food is available. The first hatched, and thus the oldest, is always the strongest and will usually secure the food that is provided; the others will weaken and die. Such a mechanism ensures that the maximum number of young survive under any circumstances. If there is enough food to go round, all will survive; if not, the number that die will depend on how short food has become. The details of the system vary from species to species. The

Silhouettes of hawk (top) and falcon (below) in flight. Note the different shapes of the wings and tail reflecting the different flight requirements of these raptors. Below: the barbules on the leading edge of the primary flight feathers of an owl are curled outwards to present a softened edge to the air currents, dampening all sound.

core is constant – and shows clearly how the same selection pressure may elicit the same response from a variety of different creatures. The response is constant for that particular environmental pressure – irrespective of the species concerned.

Such a truism underlies many of the similarities of structure, design and general biology between the birds of prey that we have discussed so far: parallel adaptations to a common requirement. So close can these parallels become that they may even suggest a closer evolutionary relationship than truly exists between the animals that show such similarities. Thus, for a long time, it was thought from evidence of comparative anatomy and physiology that the separate groups of the hawks and falcons were very closely related. Yet such a belief is in fact fallacious. Recent comparisons of blood serum proteins and of egg-white protein (albumen) have shown that the hawks and falcons are in fact only distantly related, and that the close similarities observed in structure and physiology are indeed no more than parallel adaptations to a common life-style. The assemblage of species we have included here as 'birds of prey' belong in fact to three major lines within the birds. The falcons and owls are clear and distinct groups; the kites, eagles, buzzards, harriers and 'true', short-winged hawks are all closely related evolutionarily, and placed within a single sub-family (*Accipitrinae*).

Above: female Goshawk on nest with young.
Opposite: European Eagle Owl.

At this point it would perhaps be useful to summarise the particular characteristics of these various groups. The true hawks (genus *Accipiter*) are small to medium-sized birds of swift flight, generally inhabiting woodlands or forests and preying on birds, small mammals and reptiles. All are broad-winged, long-tailed hawks with rather long legs. Males are always considerably smaller than females. Harriers (genus *Circus*) are slim hawks of medium size, with long, narrow tails, and long, slender wings, carried when gliding in a stiff V above the back. They tend to hunt in open country, quartering the ground in characteristic fashion to flush their prey. Males are again smaller than females and there is marked sexual dimorphism in colouration. The eagles and buzzards are large birds with soaring flight, which inhabit woodlands or open country, preying on mammals and reptiles caught on the ground. All are large – with a wing-span of from three to five feet – and although all can soar freely, most spend a great deal of time perched on trees, telegraph poles or rocks. The kites are the least closely related group. True kites (genus *Milvus*) are large birds with long, pointed wings and a long, deeply-forked tail. They frequent sparsely-wooded country, and human settlements, where they scavenge refuse and carrion.

These drawings (not to scale) show the type characteristics of the seven groups of raptor.

Red Kite

Common Buzzard

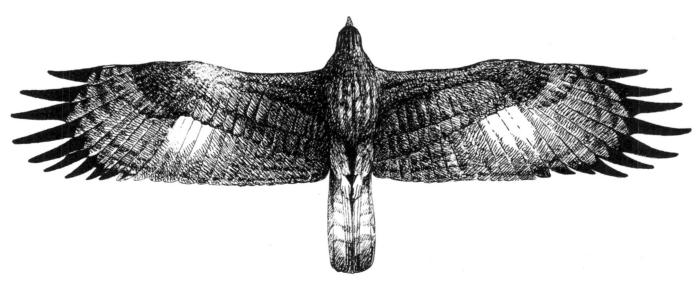

Golden Eagle

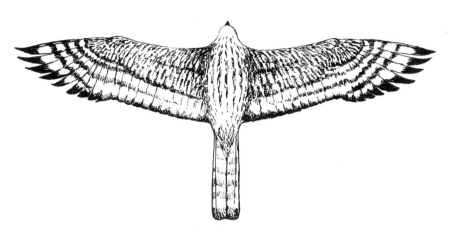

Marsh Hawk

European Sparrowhawk

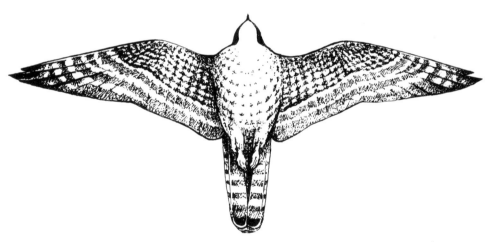

Duck Hawk

Tawny Owl

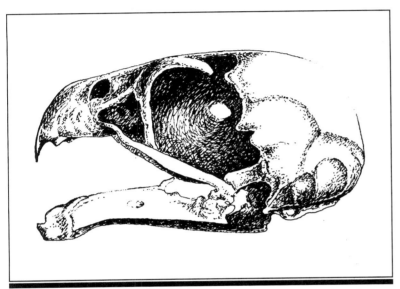

The skull of a Gyrfalcon showing the clear 'tooth' of the upper mandible.
Opposite: cock Common, or European, Kestrel on fist.

The falcons are separated into a distinct family of their own (*Falconidae*). Although they are presently retained within the same order as the hawks and hawk-like birds of prey, it seems probable that they should be further separated into a distinct order of their own. They are stocky, powerful birds with long, pointed wings and relatively short tails. Extremely swift in flight, they kill their prey, principally birds, in the air, either striking them dead with the long hind toe, or seizing them in the foot and coming to the ground with them. They have a noticeable "tooth" halfway along the upper mandible – fitting into a notch in the lower bill. This tooth can be inserted between the cervical vertebrae of prey, and used to dislocate the neck. Females are larger than males, and there is usually a distinct colour difference between the sexes. Finally, the owls are a separate order of birds altogether (*Strigiformes*) – the nocturnal counterpart of the diurnal raptors (although not all of them hunt exclusively at night). They are soft-plumaged, big-headed birds with short, broad, rounded wings and short tails. Most are arboreal, though a few species live in open grassland or in the tundra of the far north. They feed largely on ground-living rodents, earthworms and large insects, hunting by sound rather than by sight.

I referred at the outset to the uncanny fascination that birds of prey possess. Their mastery of the air, arrogant superiority, their fierce beauty have all contributed towards this aura; and somehow the forward-pointing eyes, unique within the bird world, makes man identify himself more closely with them. From very early times, birds of prey have featured in man's mythology. The haughty eagle became a symbol of might and reverence: in Greek and Roman tradition, the bird of Zeus. By contrast, owls were often birds of ill-luck or ill-omen. Pallas Athene's Owl of Wisdom, the Little Owl, became Merlin's owl of wizardry by the Dark Ages, and the owl of witchcraft in mediaeval times. The smaller birds of prey were somehow more approachable: here their fascination has led to attempts to 'man' both hawks and falcons – to work with them and use them for falconry. This sport – or 'art' as its devotees would insist – was practised in the East as long ago as 1200 BC and first introduced into England about AD 860. Over the years, a whole mystique has grown up around it, with language, methods and traditions of its own: clear evidence of the respect with which the birds were still honoured. The birds chiefly used for falconry are, among the 'long-winged hawks' (falcons), the Duck Hawk and Pigeon Hawk, and the short-winged Goshawk and Sparrowhawk. Traditionally, the fierce Goshawk was a gentleman's bird, high-

Falcon secured to the resting block. From Tractatus de Avibus, *part of the* Hortus Sanitatis *published in Venice in 1511.*

ranking ladies flew Duck Hawks, maids hunted with the little Pigeon Hawk, while youths and boys flew Sparrowhawks. All the birds used are taken from the wild as chicks ('eyasses'), when full grown but in their first plumage ('passage hawks'), or in their second plumage ('haggards'); each has its disadvantages and advantages. The hawk or falcon is tamed to the fist – largely by playing on the sense of hunger – and trained to fly from the glove and return to the 'lure' (a bunch of feathers with pieces of raw meat attached, which is swung at the end of a length of cord). The bird is fitted with 'jesses', short leather straps on the legs, which are attached by a 'swivel' to a leash, with which the bird is secured to the fist or resting 'block'. Bells are also fitted to the legs – so that by the sound of them the falconer can trace his bird if lost in thick cover. Many falconers fit their birds with stiff leather 'hoods' to blindfold them; a hooded hawk or falcon sits quiet and calm, and can be handled or moved without risk of panic.

Once the bird is trained, she may be flown: but hawks and falcons are flown in different ways. Hawks, as we have seen, are birds of woodland and scrub, whose skill lies in threading through close cover, to take their prey by surprise with a short, headlong dash. Thus a 'short-winged hawk' like a Goshawk is carried, unhooded, on the austringer's fist, held only by the jesses. When a rabbit or other suitable prey is put up, the bird will launch herself from the glove, straight at the quarry in direct pursuit. Falcons, for their part, rely when hunting on their complete mastery in the air, 'stooping' down on their quarry from above to strike at it with the long hind toe, or wearing the victim out with sheer speed of pursuit in a long chase. When falcons are flown at game – at grouse or partridges perhaps, a setter or pointer is put in to mark suitable quarry; when the game is found, the falconer removes the leash, swivel and hood of his bird and puts her in the air. She spirals up over the dog until she has 'gained her pitch'. Then she will 'wait on' overhead until the falconer 'serves' her by putting up the game below her.

While Pigeon Hawks, Duck Hawks, Goshawks and Sparrowhawks are the traditional birds of the glove, there are many other birds of prey which may be trained for falconry. Kestrels and Buzzards are easily trained – but are considered poor hunters and are thus rarely kept except by amateurs. Whatever the bird, it must be taken from the wild – and it should be remembered that in many countries this is strictly illegal. All British and American falconers must rely on imported birds to practise their 'art' and even then there are severe restrictions regarding the import and movement of such birds.

In their natural state, the owls and the diurnal birds of prey have a crucial role in the order of things. As predators, they weed out the weak, the old or the sickly within their prey populations – for it is these individuals that will prove the easiest victims. In this way they maintain the fitness of the population, ensuring that it remains strong, that weak individuals do not survive to reproduce and burden the population with their ill-adapted genes. Further, as predators, they may control the numbers of their prey. While many animal populations have sensitive mechanisms whereby they may regulate their own numbers in such a way that the population maintains an even balance with the environment which supports it, other creatures do not have intrinsic control mechanisms of this sort. For such populations it is their predators who act to regulate the numbers, and ensure that they do not increase to a level where they might damage their own environment. Finally, by reducing the numbers within their prey populations, predators may actually enhance the productivity of those populations. In reducing the numbers, they reduce any competition which might have occurred between prey individuals for food, or some other limited resource. With more food available, the surviving individuals grow better and have sufficient surplus to allow them to increase their reproductive output – the whole population 'takes heart'. Thus, by their action as predators, the raptors actually play a vital role in controlling the numbers of their prey and strengthening the stability and fitness of the population.

It is only when man is included in the picture that the birds of prey are seen in another light – competing with his interests: killing gamebird chicks, stealing his lambs or other stock. Many of these accusations have been made in ignorance, or highly exaggerated. Golden Eagles were alleged to take many newborn lambs from the highland pastures in Scotland – yet most of the beasts they took were still-born, and therefore dead before the birds arrived. The introduction of Little Owls to Britain in the 1870s was greeted with great alarm: for it was 'well-known' that they destroyed poultry and gamebird chicks. Yet scientific study has shown clearly that Little Owls prey almost exclusively on insects and small mammals, and that few birds of any kind appear in their diet. In fact, even in this context, the action of most birds of prey is generally beneficial. Most of the species on which they prey (rodents, grain-eating birds, large insects) are pests as far as man is concerned, being counter to his agricultural or other interests. Thus the raptors reduce the overall numbers of these pests and, through their regulatory action, buffer any chance of a

sudden irruption or pest plague. (As soon as the numbers of such a species start to increase, it will feature increasingly in the diet of any predator – for it is more readily available. More predators will turn to feeding upon it and the irregularity will be countered before it has any chance to develop.)

Yet these benefits are not as obvious as the havoc a hawk may wreak in a pheasant-rearing pen, and for the damage they are rightly or wrongly believed to do, birds of prey have been persecuted for centuries. In many developed countries, the populations of all birds of prey are in sad decline. In Britain, the White-tailed Eagle was exterminated by 1910 for suspected sheep-stealing; the Golden Eagle has withstood similar persecution. If farmers were responsible for the loss of the Sea Eagle, keepers accounted for the Red Kite. Up to the end of the eighteenth century, this bird was abundant throughout Britain. Then, in an era of intensive game preservation, the kite was quickly exterminated through most of its range – wiped out in England by 1870 and in Scotland by 1900. A few pairs survived in the wilder parts of central Wales, and from these few survivors, the kite – now protected as are all British birds of prey – is gradually staging a comeback. The story has been repeated again and again, in many countries and for many, many species. Persecuted, usually in ignorance, by worried farmers and over-enthusiastic keepers, the populations are decimated. The few survivors engage the attentions of egg or skin collectors – and the birds are harried towards

Above: male and female Red Kites at nest with young. Opposite: Charles St John 'collecting' a nesting male Osprey, 1848.

A young White-tailed Eagle in flight above Fair Isle.

extinction. Fortunately in many places, the raptors are now afforded complete protection. In Britain and America it is illegal to take any bird of prey, alive or dead, by any means.

With such protection, many British species began to recover their former status; then in the late 1950s populations crashed yet again: victims this time of the poisons of persistent pesticides. The first widespread use of the well-known DDT as an agricultural insecticide or seed dressing began in 1950. Between 1955 and 1956 two other chlorinated hydrocarbon pesticides, Aldrin and Dieldrin, came onto the market. Within a few years, populations of many raptors had dropped almost to extinction in many parts of the country – most obviously in intensely farmed areas where the use of these insecticides was greatest. The picture in America was similar, but greatly exaggerated, for the use of these pesticides had begun some years earlier than in Britain and the applications had been more intense. Species such as the Duck Hawk were particularly badly hit. Such dramatic consequences of the pesticides were totally unexpected: concentrations of the toxins in the preparations used as seed dressings were well below levels at which they would be poisonous to vertebrates, and anyway it seemed only to be birds of prey that were affected – birds which did not feed directly on any grain. However, it quickly became apparent that DDT, Dieldrin and Aldrin were persistent chemicals that did not readily denature, so persistent that they rapidly permeated all parts of the

ecological system. Furthermore they accumulated up food chains. A pigeon feeding on DDT-treated grain, takes in large quantities of the toxin. DDT is removed from circulation in the animal's body and deposited in fat. Thus, over a period of time, a pigeon might accumulate considerable quantities of DDT within its body although these might not be sufficient to kill it. A Duck Hawk will kill and eat many pigeons during its life. If each of these contains quantities of DDT, all the toxins that they have separately taken in will accumulate in the body of the raptor. The effect is additive. Since at each step up the chain an individual feeds on large numbers of individuals of the previous level, any persistent toxin is accumulated and concentrated along the chain. And the result? Mass deaths of the predators at the end of the chain. But the deaths were only a part of the story. Breeding success of many raptors declined: eggshells seemed somehow thinner, and more susceptible to breakage. Many eggs that were laid proved infertile. It was found that the adult birds had started to peck at and eat their own eggs and young. Curious effects – explained only when it emerged that both adult birds and eggs were loaded with pesticides. Clearly, even in quantities too low to cause actual death, the pesticides had insidious sublethal effects. Sparrowhawks and Duck Hawks almost vanished from the countryside; other species were not far behind them.

Both Britain and America have imposed voluntary bans on the use of persistent pesticides, using instead chemicals such as pyrethrum, which do not have the same side-effects. Gradually the birds of prey are making a comeback again, although the effects of the pesticides of the 50s are still only too much in evidence, hampering a rapid recovery. The average number of chicks surviving from 100 Sparrowhawk nests in Britain between 1956 and 1970 was 172; before 1950 the figure was nearer 400. Happily other species, such as the Common Kestrel, have shown themselves more resilient and are back almost to their former numbers.

The ignorant persecution of large birds of prey by farmers and gamekeepers has been stopped. The crippling damage caused by the chlorinated hydrocarbon pesticides, arrested. Gradually it is appreciated that the raptors have their place in the system and, on balance, do considerably more good than harm. With this realisation came the first positive attempts at conservation. The only British bird of prey to be completely extirpated was the Earn – the White-tailed Eagle – and attempts are being made to reintroduce this species. A number of young eagles were released in Fair Isle in 1968; further release attempts have since been made

Eagle soaring. A drawing by J. C. Harrison.

Above: wood engraving by Thomas Bewick of a Little Owl. Opposite: a page of owls from H. Ruysch's Theatrum Universale Omnium Animalium.

on the island of Rhum in the Hebrides. Programmes of protection have had their successes, too. The Red Kite, down to eight or nine pairs in Britain in 1905, has struggled back so that there were some twenty-six pairs recorded breeding in 1972. In America special recovery teams have been appointed to work towards the protection and re-establishment of the Duck Hawk and the Californian Condor.

But protection and reintroduction are not enough; conservation attempts must be positive. One of the easiest ways to cause a decline in a population is to make inroads upon its chosen habitat. Such encroachment of habitat seems to have been a major contributing factor to the decline of Osprey populations in many parts of America, exacerbating a situation where populations were already affected by pesticides. The erosion of timber by rivers and lakesides hampered the reovery of the birds even when the effects of the pesticides themselves began to diminish. Now, numbers of Ospreys in many areas have at last begun to

increase again, as several National Forests set up Osprey Management areas where timber use of the area is altered to minimise disturbance to the breeding fish-hawks. Where nesting habitat is disappearing, artificial nesting sites are being provided: such nesting platforms can be seen all along the Atlantic coast, in every state from South Carolina to New York, and, although the Ospreys may have evolved as a tree-nesting species, they are proving themselves very adaptable to these man-made structures. Indeed, over two-thirds of the 1,450 Ospreys breeding in Chesapeake Bay are nesting on artificial platforms and there is even some evidence to suggest that birds nesting on these man-made platforms are more successful than those nesting in the traditional trees! The Ospreys' future seems secure, even if a low natural recruitment rate, further reduced by the lingering effects of pesticides, means that recovery will be slow. But the example serves to emphasise that an essential part of any conservation scheme must be habitat preservation. Conservation for our birds of prey is essential – not merely for aesthetic reasons, because these are beautiful birds, wild, untamed and swift-flying, but because these beleaguered species truly play a beneficial part in the system, maintaining the stability and controlling the pests.

This book collects together thirty-five paintings of birds of prey by Gareth Parry, representing some thirty different species. Reflecting Gareth Parry's own experience with the birds of his Welsh home, all are essentially European in their distribution, with over twenty breeding in the British Isles. However, many also occur, or have close counterparts, in the New World; and five species of purely American distribution have been included in this edition. With each plate is paired a text which attempts to balance the painting in providing background information about the distribution, habits and general biology of the bird portrayed and, where relevant, its American counterpart. Handbook fact is tempered by anecdote, by biological curiosity or peculiarity of the species in question, in the hope that the texts and pictures in complement will make these birds of prey live.

Rory Putman
Southampton, 1979

Female Snowy Owl with young.

HABITAT & DISTRIBUTION

Opposite: the Duck Hawk lives in desolate upland country such as this.
Overleaf, left: mixed deciduous woodland – home of the European Sparrowhawk and Tawny Owl.
Overleaf, right: coniferous forest is the typical haunt of the Scops Owl.

Eagles, Hawks & Falcons

Breeding range is shown in dark grey; winter range of migratory species in pale grey.

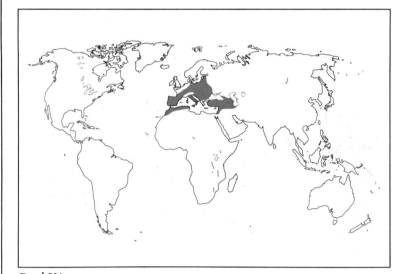

Red Kite

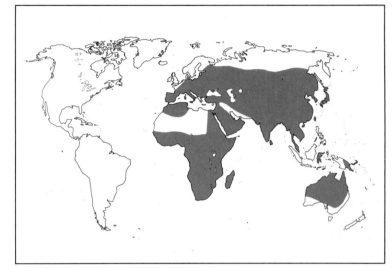

Black Kite

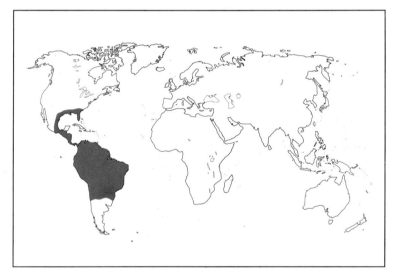

Swallow-tailed Kite

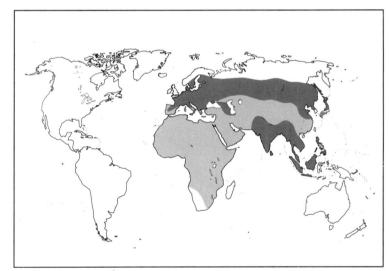

Honey Buzzard

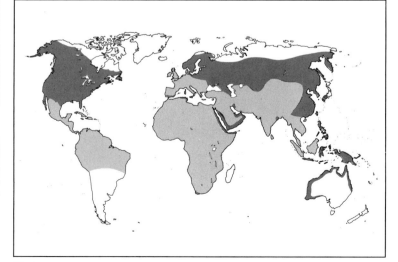

Osprey

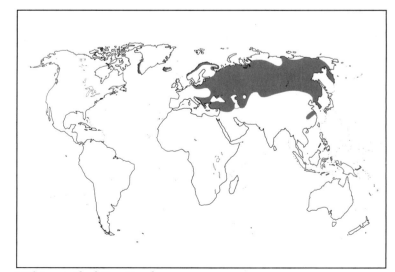

White-tailed Sea Eagle

Eagles, Hawks & Falcons

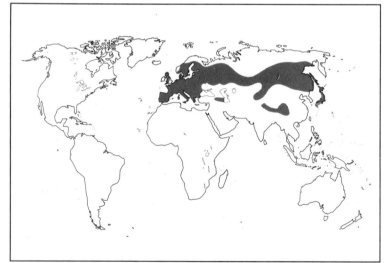

Bald Eagle

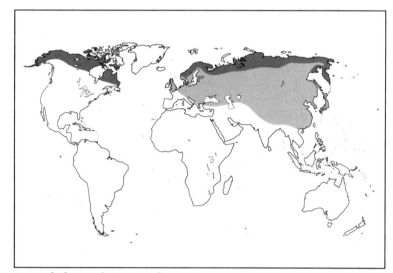

Golden Eagle

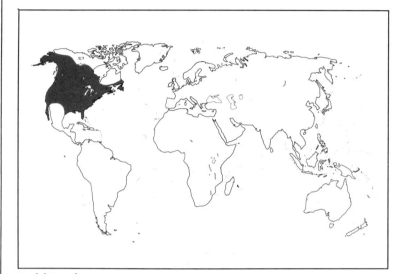

Common Buzzard

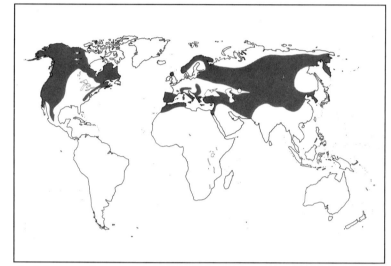

Rough-legged Buzzard

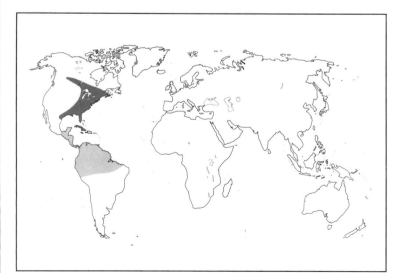

Broad-winged Hawk

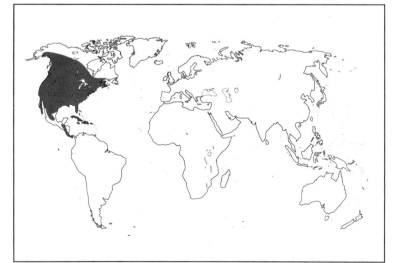

Red-tailed Hawk

Eagles, Hawks & Falcons

Breeding range is shown in dark grey; winter range of
migratory species in pale grey.

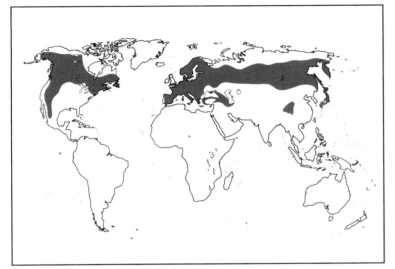

Goshawk

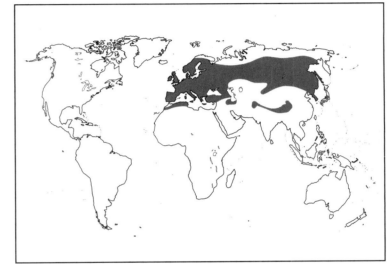

European Sparrowhawk

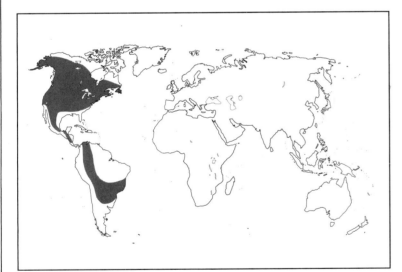

Sharp-shinned Hawk

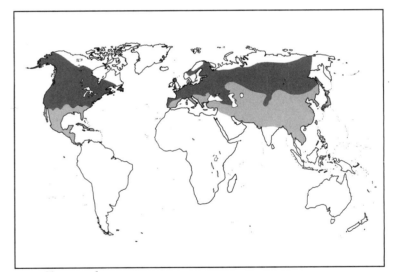

Marsh Hawk

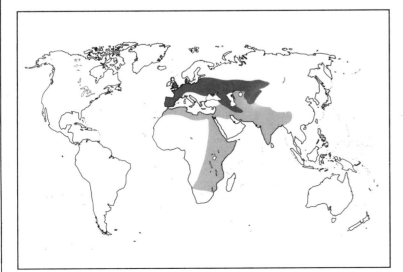

Montagu's Harrier

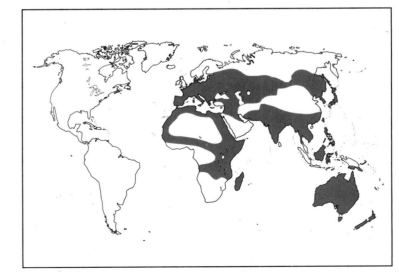

Marsh Harrier

Eagles, Hawks & Falcons

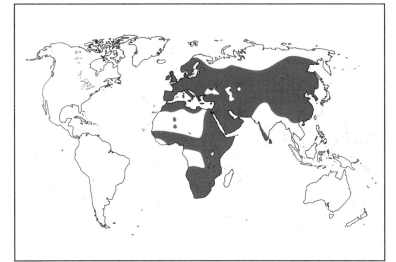

Gyrfalcon

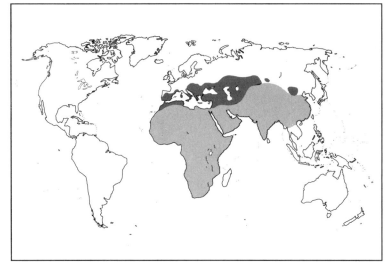

Duck Hawk

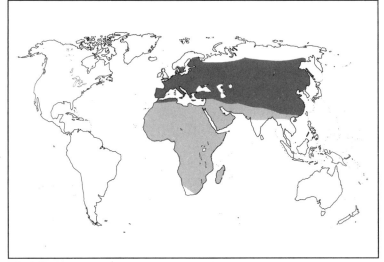

Hobby

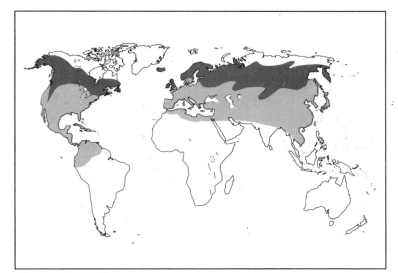

Pigeon Hawk

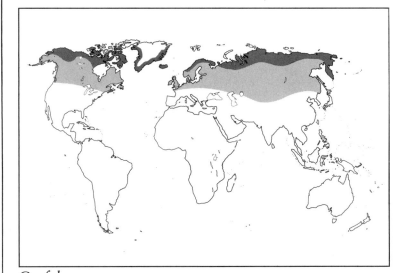

Common Kestrel

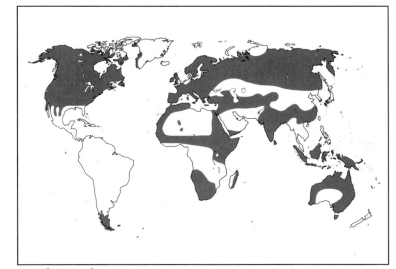

Lesser Kestrel

Falcons & Owls

Breeding range is shown in dark grey; winter range of migratory species in pale grey.

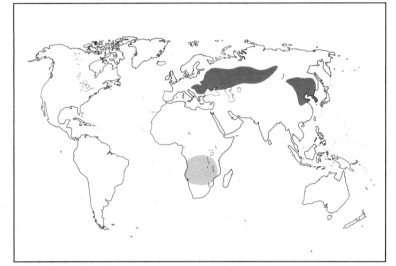

Red-footed Falcon

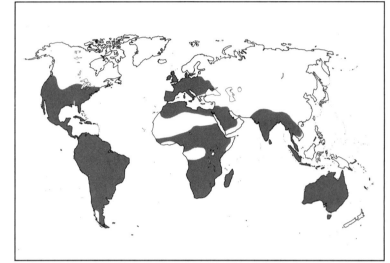

Barn Owl

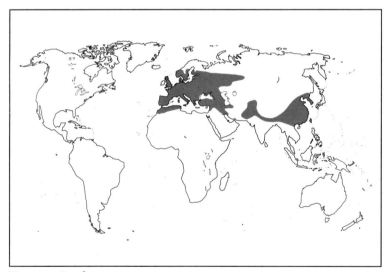

Tawny Owl

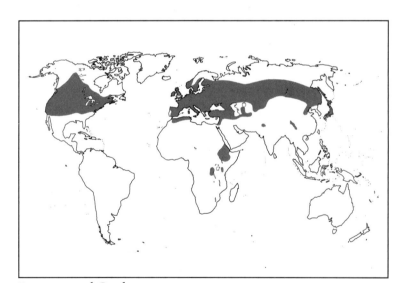

Long-eared Owl

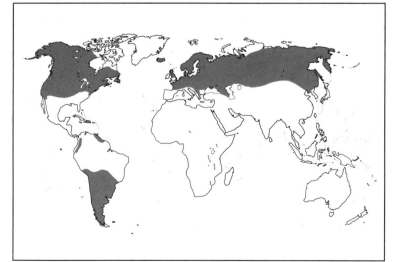

Short-eared Owl

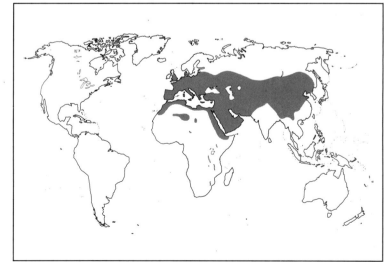

Little Owl

Owls

Eagle Owl: the Great Horned Owl (*Bubo Virginianus*) is the American equivalent of this European bird.

Scops Owl: birds occurring below the dotted line on the map are often considered to be a separate species – the African Scops Owl (*Otus capensis*).

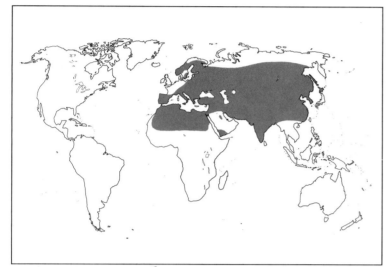

Eagle Owl

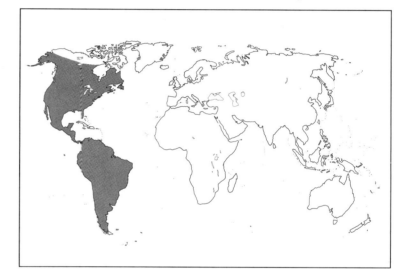

Great Horned Owl

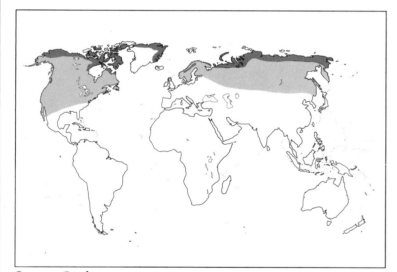

Snowy Owl

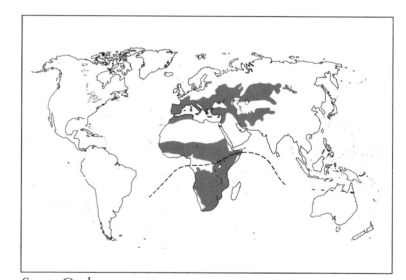

Scops Owl

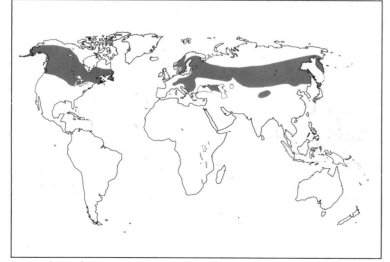

Boreal Owl

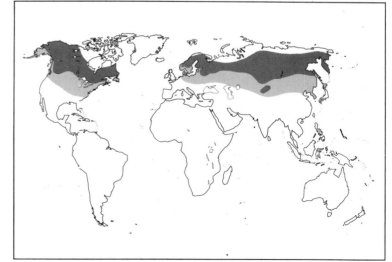

Hawk Owl

Left: the remote eyrie of the Golden Eagle.
Below: Golden Eagle by Thomas Bewick.

Left: moorland habitat of the Pigeon Hawk and Marsh Hawk.
Below: wood engraving of a Marsh Hawk by Thomas Bewick.

Opposite: male Osprey bringing fish to mate.

EAGLES, HAWKS & FALCONS

Plate 1. Red Kite (Milvus milvus)

The Red Kite is a large kite, easily recognised by its generally reddish colour, the long wings angled back from the wrist, and long, deeply-forked tail.

Broadly distributed across Europe and Asia Minor, North-west Africa and the Canary and Cape Verde Islands, it is a bird of mixed habitat, for it requires tall trees for nesting and open spaces – moorlands, parkland or farmland – for hunting. Measuring some twenty-four inches, it has a pale head: white, tinged rufous and streaked with blackish brown; the sides of the head, chin and throat are white, again streaked with black. The neck and upper back are dark brown, but chestnut edges to the feathers produce the effect of a red shawl covering the darker, lower back. The kite has a clear chestnut tail tipped with buff, with black bars or spots on the outer feathers only. The underside – breast and belly – maintains the reddish colouration, being chestnut streaked with black.

Hunting over open lowland country, the Red Kite feeds on small mammals up to the size of a large rat or weasel, young gamebirds, and other birds. It can cope with birds up to the size of a wood-pigeon, and is agile enough in flight to be able to catch such prey on the wing. Like most kites, however, it has a catholic taste, and will also eat frogs, snakes and lizards, stranded fish and carrion. Indeed, in historical times, over most of its range, scavenging habits gave it a role now more usually played by the Black Kite (*Milvus migrans*): that of town scavenger. Certainly in Britain, up to the end of the eighteenth century, the Red Kite was abundant in the streets of larger towns. Brown, in his book *British Birds of Prey* notes: "One sixteenth century traveller, Le Cluse, likened its numbers to those of Black Kites in Cairo. Assuming that the Egyptians were at least as insanitary in 1570 as they are today, that must have been common indeed." However, it has now lost this role over most of its range, presumably through competition with the bolder and more agile Black Kite, and only the Cape Verdes race remains directly associated with man as street-cleaner.

In the breeding season the kites withdraw to woodland haunts of tall, deciduous timber. The same breeding areas are used year after year by the same pair, or a succession of pairs. The males arrive first at the breeding territory and call to passing females. Courtship display consists chiefly of soaring and calling over the chosen site, often at a great height. Kites do not usually build a nest of their own, but take over, and add to, the nests of other birds. Building is usually done in the late evening and early morning, and the birds continue to add to the nest right through the season, even when eggs have been laid and chicks hatched. The nest is characteristically 'decorated' with rags and paper, scraps of fur and dung. The adults are not strictly territorial and, surprisingly, may occasionally breed in a sort of loose, mixed colony with Black Kites, where they occur together. The female broods the eggs, while the male hunts for her and for himself. However, she sits close only after the eggs are hatched, and until that time often leaves the nest to hunt for herself, or to join the male in soaring flights above their wood.

In Britain, the Red Kite is now extremely rare. At the end of the eighteenth century, an era of intensive game preservation began in this country and although until that time it was a very abundant species, as a potential predator of gamebird chicks the Red Kite was quickly exterminated over most of its former range. It was wiped out in England by 1870 and in Scotland by 1900. Only a few pairs survived in the wilder parts of Wales – unkeepered territory – while occasional reports were heard of Red Kites on Dartmoor. But from an estimated eight or nine pairs in 1905, the Red Kite is fighting back: it is estimated that there are now some thirty pairs breeding each year in Wales, and numbers are still increasing.

Red Kite

Plate 2. Black Kite (Milvus migrans)

Black Kite by Joseph Wolf, from John Gould's Birds of Great Britain *volume I, first published in 1873.*

Known also as the Common, or Pariah Kite, the Black Kite is the habitual scavenger of poorer towns in the Old World. Indeed, for many travellers recalling the heat, the squalor, the indescribable smell of poverty of African and Eastern towns, the picture would not be complete without the Black Kite. In fact it is one of the world's commonest and most successful birds of prey, ranging throughout Europe, Africa and the Middle East, India and Southern Asia, east as far as South China and south to New Guinea and Australia. Northern populations are strongly migratory in winter, moving south to the warmer parts of their range, and all races are migratory to some extent (hence the name, *Milvus migrans*).

Recognised as a dark brown to black bird with a lighter, grey head, and the long, angled wings and long, forked tail of the kites, the Black Kite, because of its adaptability, is able to colonise a wide variety of terrains. It is a successful opportunist, able to make a living under almost any circumstances. It will feed on anything it can get, from insects caught in flight, to small mammals, fish, frogs, young poultry and carrion. It is also piratical, pursuing other birds, particularly other kites, in the hope of making them drop their prey, which it will then seize. Black Kites often follow plagues of mice or locusts, and are quick to gather at a grass fire, hovering in large groups over the advancing flames to pick up escaping or wounded prey. Where not commensal with man, they typically prefer lightly-wooded country with open areas and a few big trees. It is, however, the bird of prey most reliant on man's activities, and it is usually far more numerous in and around towns and cities than in open country. Indeed, in some areas it occurs in its thousands, breeding in trees in the streets and snatching food from roadways and rubbish tips.

Always gregarious – not just when forced together by common exploitation of human refuse – Black Kites tend to congregate in favoured spots: open grassy banks on which they can sun themselves, on sandbanks or stream edges to bathe. They also form communal roosts, and when on migration, move in large flocks.

Like the Red Kite, Black Kites return to established breeding sites year after year. Although it is not known for certain, it seems likely that the birds pair for life; certainly they often arrive at the breeding ground already paired, and nuptial displays, confirming a pair bond, are often seen in winter migrating flocks. The courtship display usually involves circling and twisting pursuits of one bird by the other; the male, who usually flies a little above and behind the female, may dive down on his mate, who turns on her back to present her claws to his. Occasionally the two birds may come together and grip claws, and then cartwheel to earth together, separating just above the ground. The nest is built in a tree, usually on top of a previous nest, or that of some other bird, and, like that of the Red Kite, is nearly always 'decorated' with bits of rag, paper, dry skin, bones and other scraps. While the female incubates the two or three eggs, the male frequently spends a great deal of his time perched near the nest in a tree.

Black Kite

Plate 3. Swallow-tailed Kite
(Elanoides forficatus)

The Swallow-tailed Kite is a New World species – the sole member of its genus *(Elanoides)* and only distantly related to the other kites. It is a large bird with long, pointed wings, and a long, deeply-forked tail; the deep cleft – far deeper than that of any other bird of prey – is completely distinctive.

Widely distributed over tropical and subtropical America, the Swallow-tailed Kite breeds from the eastern United States, through Mexico and Central America, down through most of South America to northern Argentina. In the United States it is now common only in southern Florida, although a few breed along the Atlantic coast to South Carolina. Two distinct sub-species are recognised, *Elanoides forficatus forficatus* from the southern United States to north Mexico, and *E. f. yetapa*, from southern Mexico through South America. In all parts of its range the Kite is highly migratory: most of the birds north of Panama migrate to South America in the autumn, while even in the southern part of its range the species shows extensive local migrations.

Characteristic of forest country – lowland swamps of cypress or pine forest in the United States and rain forest in South America – the Swallow-tailed Kite is an elegant creature with a snowy white head and neck, bluish black upper parts and tail, with a marked bloom. (The two subspecies are distinguished by the colour of this gloss on the mantle, which is purplish red in the typical *E. f. forficatus*, green in the southern *E. f. yetapa.*) The underparts, including the underside of the wings, are also clear white, making a marked contrast with the black wing and tail quills when viewed from below. The most distinctive feature is the long, forked tail, which is often spread but also opened and closed in flight like a pair of scissors to give manoeuvrability.

Although occasionally found perched, the Kite is more usually seen on the wing, where its size and agility give it a superb elegance. It is capable of sustained flight, and indeed spends most of its time in the air, seeming to live almost entirely on the wing. Its diet is composed largely of insects, which it seizes with a sudden grab by one or other foot and eats in flight, but the Kite also feeds on the eggs and nestlings of other birds, arboreal snakes and lizards. This prey, too, is taken in flight; the bird never alights. When nest-robbing, it may pause and flutter above the eggs or chicks for a few moments, but frequently it snatches away the entire nest, and eats the fledglings as it flies along. It prefers exposed nests but has been known to sweep down between the trees to prey on nests only a few feet from the ground.

Swallow-tailed Kites are quite social, though more especially on migration, and may often be seen feeding together. In common with other species of kite, too, there is a tendency towards social nesting, and it is not uncommon to see several pairs nesting within a few hundred yards of each other. Nests are built in the tops of tall, slender trees, on the edges of woods or in open areas, so that the birds can approach easily, and drop onto the nest. The structure is built of dead twigs that – true to the Kites' complete commitment to an airborne existence – are snapped off in flight. Suitable twigs are transferred to the bill and carefully balanced for transport back to the nest; twigs that are too small are dropped. The nest is lined with 'Spanish moss', and more moss is added to the nest throughout incubation. The nests measure fifteen to twenty inches across and are about a foot in depth. There is little courtship display; two or, less commonly, three eggs are laid from mid-March to mid-April, and incubation is shared by both birds.

Swallow–tailed Kite

Plate 4. Honey Buzzard (Pernis apivorus)

Wash drawing of a Honey Buzzard by Eric Ennion.
Reproduced by kind permission of Sir Peter Scott.

The Honey Buzzard – despite its name – is strictly not a buzzard at all, but a member of the Kite family. However, it has long, broad wings like a true buzzard, and although it spends less time in the air, can soar freely, and can occasionally be seen to hover. The rest of its common name is also something of a misnomer, for the Honey Buzzard rarely eats honey. It is indeed a predator of the nests of bees and wasps, but attacks them to feed upon the insects themselves, both adults and larvae, rather than on any honey that may be in the nests.

While Honey Buzzards will also prey on small mammals, reptiles, frogs and large insects, a very large proportion of the food does come from these attacks on wasps' and bees' nests. Many characteristics of the birds' behaviour and ecology reflect this very specialised and restricted diet. It is for example, a woodland bird, with a preference for mature stands, particularly deciduous woodland, where there are likely to be found the nests of the wasps and bees on which it preys. Further, although as noted above, the Honey Buzzard can fly freely, it in fact spends little time in the air, preferring to walk and hop about on the ground like a large crow. When on the ground it uses its feet to dig out wasps' and bees' nests, eating both adults and larvae: catching the adults dexterously around their middle and ripping off the sting before swallowing them whole. When excavating a nest, the bird will dig quite deep, continuing until most of its body is underground.

In its general appearance, also, the Honey Buzzard is adapted to its special diet. Clearly it has strong legs and feet for digging, but in addition, the sides of the head and the forehead are covered with fine, grey, scale-like feathers to protect the head from stings. For the rest, it usually has a dark head and dark brown back with underparts essentially white or buff but obscured by dark streaks and bars. The long tail is dark brown with a white or buff tip, and just behind this is a broad black band supported by two or three other black bands.

Honey Buzzards are found in deciduous woodlands, notably beech woodland, in Europe, Asia, India and Indonesia. Northern races are migratory, and visitors to Britain leave in winter. Breeding pairs set up large territories at the beginning of spring, for the parents may have to forage well over two miles from the nest for food. Their display involves a great many mutual soaring flights above the breeding site, during which the male may dive down and swoop up again, and at intervals rise steeply and hover, clapping his wings together above his back for a few quick strokes before diving again on the female. This wing-clapping is distinctive to the species.

The nest is built in a large tree, often on the foundation of an old nest of some other bird. Incubation of the one to three eggs is shared by both parents. In most species of birds, as the female comes into reproductive condition, she loses the feathers from her breast and belly; the skin becomes highly sensitive and richly supplied with surface blood vessels. This 'brood patch' is clearly an adaptation for brooding both eggs and young, and giving them the necessary warmth for survival. Males do not normally develop such a patch. However, in Honey Buzzards, where the male takes on a significant share of the incubation, the male, too, rather unusually, develops a true brood patch. When the young hatch, they are fed exclusively on the larvae of bee or wasp combs. The insects' nest is ultimately discarded, and Honey Buzzard nests are easy to recognise from the pieces of comb left littered all over them. After ten days to a fortnight, the fledglings can take larger prey, but, as always, the prey is that which the parents can catch during their forays on the ground.

Honey Buzzard

Plate 5. Osprey (Pandion haliaetus)

Male Osprey stalling to alight on nest.

The Osprey gives us one of the best examples from amongst the birds of prey, of how finely attuned form may become to function. For this is a fish hawk, spending most of its time by water and feeding almost exclusively on fish, and much of its structure reflects this way of life. Ospreys have large feet with long toes, the lower surfaces of which are covered with sharp spicules to help them grip their slippery prey. The feathers are dense and compact – particularly on the breast – reducing the impact when the bird plunges into the water after fish, and helping to prevent the plumage from becoming waterlogged. As a further aquatic adaptation, the horny 'cere', the lump at the base of the bill, is enlarged and can be drawn down to cover the nostrils as the hawk dives.

Ospreys are large hawks, the size of small eagles, found almost all over the world, although they tend to be rarer in the southern hemisphere than in the north, and have never been proved to breed there regularly except in Australia and the nearby islands. More northerly populations, and those farther south migrate to warmer climates in the winter. Both sexes are alike, having dark-brown upper parts with a faintly purplish tinge, and underparts white with pale-brown lower throat and breast. The crown of the head and nape are buff with dark streaks; separating this pale nape from the white throat, is a broad, dark stripe which runs from the forepart of the crown, back through the eye. Except during migration, Ospreys are always associated with water, by rivers and lakes or on sea coasts, and spend much of their time perched, hunched, in trees. The birds may be recognised as easily by these habits as by plumage.

At intervals, an Osprey may leave its perch to fly out over the water on long, narrow wings to try to catch fish. When hunting, it flies at a height of between fifty and a hundred feet; on sighting a fish, it may hover briefly with tail spread, wings fanning rapidly, before plunging into the water feet and head foremost, wings held arched and sharply angled, above the back. The bird may disappear completely under water or may just touch the surface. The hunting technique varies, and the hawk may plunge straight into the water from normal flight, without first hovering above its prey, but whatever its style, the Osprey is extraordinarily adept, and may be successful in taking a fish on as many as ninety percent of dives.

Although found near any water body, Ospreys are commonest on sea coasts, less frequent on inland waters. The nest is built on a crag or in a solitary tree, and the same nest is returned to year after year. Repaired each year, the nest therefore becomes very large, and, in its isolated position, very obvious. After a typical display flight of dives and upward swoops, three eggs are laid. The female plays the greater role in incubation, although the male takes a considerable share – up to thirty percent of the time. Curiously, in America, the female always incubates alone.

In much of Europe and North America, the numbers of Ospreys have declined drastically in recent years, due in large part to the effects of pesticides. In Britain, the Osprey was extinct by 1910 – before ever pesticides were widely used. In this case, it was the old story of decimation of once numerous and widespread populations by gamekeepers, with the *coup de grâce* delivered by the intensive activities of egg and skin collectors. In America populations in most areas fell dramatically in the late 1950s, and in this case it is clear that persistent pesticides were implicated. Birds on the South Atlantic coast were relatively unaffected, and this coastline now boasts the largest concentration of nesting Ospreys in the world, with in excess of 2,100 pairs. Elsewhere in the country, too, the decline in numbers is abating, and in many areas populations have recently begun to increase again, in response not only to a ban on the use of chlorinated hydrocarbon pesticides like DDT, but also to an intensive positive conservation effort. In Scotland, too, the Ospreys have returned. The first successful nesting by a single pair of birds was recorded in 1957. Since that time, other pairs have established themselves in the area, and there are now five or six pairs of Ospreys known to be breeding regularly in Scotland in very closely-guarded nest sites.

Osprey

Plate 6. White-tailed Sea Eagle
(Haliaeetus albicilla)

Engraving by Thomas Bewick of the White-tailed Sea Eagle.

The genus *Haliaeetus* to which the White-tailed Sea Eagles belong is a group of large or very large eagles, with long, broad wings and usually short tails. The genus includes *Haliaeetus leucocephalus*, the Bald or American Eagle, on the North American continent.

The White-tailed Eagle is a huge, grey-brown eagle with a strikingly white, wedge-shaped tail and bare, yellow feet. It is found mainly in Greenland and locally in Europe and Asia. Its range formerly included the Highlands and islands of north-west Scotland, and attempts have recently been made to re-establish the eagles in these areas. Throughout its range, the White-tailed Eagle is chiefly a bird of sea coasts, large river valleys and inland lakes. The birds feed on mammals: the rabbits and hares of the short turf of cliff tops or rocky islands, fish, and a large variety of water birds. When hunting, they fly low over the ground and attempt to catch their prey by surprise, for they cannot catch fast-flying birds on the wing. When after fish, they usually try to snatch them from the water surface, and rarely plunge right into the water like an Osprey. In the breeding season, the diet is composed of these different elements with from fifty to sixty percent of the food made up of water birds, twenty-five to thirty percent fish, and the remainder mammals and carrion. Although frequently accused of taking lambs, and exterminated in Britain largely for that reason, it is probable that most of the lambs taken, or on which eagles are observed to be feeding, were already dead.

Sea Eagles pair for life and except where winter conditions force them to migrate, remain together in their breeding territory all year round. The size of the individual range varies with the type of terrain and abundance of food, but is usually from twenty to sixty square miles – not all of which is necessarily used. Within this area, the eagles spend most of their time perched on trees or crags, where they sit motionless for hours. When pairs remain in the breeding territory, they become very attached to the actual nest site, roosting in the vicinity every night. Each pair has several nests – up to eleven within one territory – and may use different ones in different years. The nests are built in large solitary trees, usually conifers, and are added to year by year, until they may become five or six feet thick and as much across. The importance of the nest site to the pair is emphasised by the fact that renovations and additions to the nest are made throughout the year. Nuptial displays, too, may occur at any time, although they increase in intensity towards the breeding season.

One or two eggs are laid, occasionally three. The female begins to sit as soon as the first egg has been laid, and continues to do so for most of the incubation period although the male may relieve her when she is off the nest killing prey. The female has to feed herself throughout; the male only occasionally brings food to the nest for her. The eaglets hatch at intervals over a period of some days, so that, as in many birds of prey, the nest contains young of a variety of ages. This is an adaptation so that the broodsize may be adjusted to that level at which there is sufficient food available to support the chicks. If food is scarce, the youngest chicks die, since they are unable to compete successfully with their siblings for whatever food is available. The number that die is related to the food supply. Thus the parents rear the maximum number of young that available food can support; if they continued to share the decreased food amongst all the chicks, all would suffer and probably all would die.

White-tailed Sea Eagle

Plate 7. Bald Eagle
(Haliaeetus leucocephalus)

The Bald, or American, Eagle is another typical sea-eagle: the New World counterpart of the White-tailed Eagle *(Haliaeetus albicilla)*. The heraldic bird of the United States, the Bald Eagle is found throughout the North American continent, south to southern Florida and Mexico. Although much reduced over large parts of its former range, it is still common in Alaska and northern British Columbia; always it is more or less restricted to the coast, and the edges of large lakes and rivers.

A large, brownish black eagle, with a snowy white head and tail, bright yellow bill, eyes and feet, it is a most impressive and extraordinarily beautiful bird. The white head – from which the eagle derives its apparent 'baldness' when viewed from a distance – is characteristic of adult birds only. Immatures are uniformly brown, and take on adult plumage only gradually, attaining the full white head and tail only at four or five years of age.

Bald Eagles frequent rocky coasts, or sparsely wooded lakes or river-sides inland. Partial migrants, they forsake their breeding grounds in the autumn and congregate in considerable numbers at favoured wintering areas where food is available. At all times of year they are characteristically found soaring majestically above their haunts or sitting in a solitary tree along the water's edge; in winter there may be upwards of twenty birds in any one tree and immatures roost gregariously even during the breeding season. Much time is spent sitting motionless on such a favoured perch, scarcely moving a muscle, for when food is abundant the eagles do not need to spend more than three or four hours a day hunting.

Bald Eagles feed on fish, waterbirds and mammals; while they may prefer live prey – and certainly catch many live fish and waterfowl – they eat a great deal of carrion. In exactly the same way that White-tailed Eagles were exterminated in Britain for suspected sheep-stealing, the Bald Eagle has been persecuted in many parts of America for its alleged depredations on domestic livestock – especially lambs – and salmon. In Alaska bounties have been paid on literally thousands of eagles, which accounts in some measure for the reduction in numbers over much of its range. But again, it is probable that the lambs or salmon taken were dead or dying, and the eagles were merely feeding on them as carrion. Over most of their range the staple diet is dead or dying fish, or mammal carrion, but the eagles also snatch live fish from near the surface of the water, and in some areas take a large number of sea birds. Occasionally, two birds will join forces to tire out and catch a larger sea bird. The birds are also piratical and may frequently harass Ospreys, forcing them to drop their fish, which the Bald Eagle then catches.

Bald Eagles pair for life, and return from the wintering areas to their traditional nesting territory at the start of the breeding season. The pair may engage in various spectacular courtship flights: locking talons in mid-air and plummeting down together for several hundred feet in a series of somersaults. The nest – the largest of all nests built by a single pair of birds – is sited in a

Head of the Bald Eagle.

commanding position in a large tree. It is built of twigs and sticks, and is added to year after year, until it may measure eight or nine feet across and twelve feet in depth, and until the burden of the nest may actually kill the tree in which it is built. The nest is lined with grass or other vegetation, and one to three (usually two) eggs are laid within a deep cup in this lining with an interval of several days between each. Although the female undertakes most of the incubation, the male may take a turn at least at some nests. Frequently, two or even three eaglets are reared, although, as with other eagles, when food is scarce there is much competition between the chicks and the weaker may be killed. Both parents feed the young, which remain in the nest for ten to eleven weeks.

The reduction in numbers of Bald Eagles, through persecution and encroachment of breeding habitat, has been exacerbated in recent years by a decrease in nesting success in some areas. In 1962 only two or three of about fifty active nests in the middle Atlantic states brought off young – and this may be due to the effects of pesticides. Despite this decline, the Bald Eagle's future is relatively secure; winter concentrations along rivers near the coast of Alaska may number 3,000–4,000 eagles along one ten-mile stretch.

Bald Eagle

Plate 8. Golden Eagle (Aquila chrysaetos)

A large, dark-brown eagle with golden tips to the feathers of crown and nape, the Golden Eagle is the characteristic eagle of mountainous country throughout its range, occurring over a large part of the northern hemisphere, north to the treeline, south to North Africa, Arabia and the Himalayas in the Old World, and to Mexico in America. It is perhaps the most abundant eagle of its size, due both to the extent of its range and the great areas of mountainous country within this. It is a typical eagle, with long wings and a broad tail for soaring, powerful legs and talons – the legs feathered right to the toes – and a heavy beak. The colouring is somewhat variable; many birds have lighter underparts, even becoming buff on thighs and feet, and some Scottish and north-east American birds have distinctive white 'epaulettes' on the wings.

Golden Eagles are superb fliers, and spend hours soaring above their territories in effortless flight. Sailing above a ridge with partially closed wings, or circling to rise in spirals on currents of air above a bluff, an eagle may appear to be moving very slowly, but this lazy movement is deceptive and the bird is in fact travelling at considerable speed and covering a great deal of ground on its six or seven foot wing span. When shifting position from one ridge to another it may reach speeds of up to 120 miles per hour as it first gains height and then glides swiftly away to sweep up again with perfect timing to establish itself in a new thermal. The home range of a pair of Golden Eagles may extend from 11,000 to 18,000 acres. However, they rarely hunt over the whole of the range equally, having definitely preferred sites where they are usually found.

Most prey is taken on the ground, although occasionally large birds – ducks, geese, large gamebirds – may be killed in the air. The normal method of hunting is surprisingly hawk-like, quartering hill slopes very slowly, working along just below a ridge and swinging over it from time to time to drop suddenly on prey surprised in the open. Golden Eagles show a strong preference for feeding on mammals: rabbits, hares, deer calves, and in different parts of its range, mammalian prey makes up from seventy to one hundred percent of the total diet. Where gamebirds are abundant, these also form a considerable portion of the diet. Carrion is also taken, and in winter, may become the staple food. Although Golden Eagles have been accused of killing many lambs, and persecuted for this in many areas, there is no doubt that this is an example of the eagles' carrion habits and that most lambs taken are already dead. In fact on balance, Golden Eagles are generally beneficial, removing large rodents and potential predators, and clearing up carcases.

Although in the more northerly parts of their range the birds are partial migrants, moving south after the end of the breeding season, in more temperate areas they remain resident throughout the year. For such residents, the nest site remains the focal point of the territory all year round, and nuptial displays can be seen in almost any month. The most usual display is an undulating flight: a series of dives and upward swoops interspersed with a few wing beats at the top of each swoop. Otherwise the birds may soar together over a ridge; the male may dive towards the female who rolls on her back and presents her claws to him in a display characteristic of many raptors. The nest or 'eyrie' is built on a ledge of a crag or in a solitary tree. Each pair has a number of these nests, all, or some of which they use in rotation; often they use one of these most of the time. Nests on ledges start out as little more than shallow scrapes with perhaps a ring of branches around them and some lining. But after a number of years of repair and re-use they become huge structures as much as eight to ten feet across and three to four feet deep. Tree nests are usually even bigger, the largest recorded being some seventeen feet deep and four foot across. The pair will commonly build up two or three such nests each year before finally choosing one.

The female lays two eggs with an interval of three or four days between them. As do other birds of prey, she starts to incubate as soon as the first egg is laid and thus the young hatch at an interval of several days. In other birds of prey, the youngest chicks are the ones to die first if food becomes scarce. In Golden Eagles, in eighty percent of cases where two young hatch, the older eaglet actually kills the younger.

Top left: drawing by J. C. Harrison of an eagle gliding.
Above: Golden Eagle at nest with young.

Golden Eagle

Plate 9. Common Buzzard (Buteo buteo)

A large, dark-brown hawk with a barred tail, some one and a half to two pounds in weight, the Buzzard is, so to speak, the hawks' answer to the eagles. Buzzards occur throughout the Palearctic region – Europe and Asia. They are soaring hawks with broad, rounded wings, noticeably short necks and longish, rounded tails which are usually spread in flight.

Buzzards are woodland birds, inhabiting forests of all types provided there is also some open ground. Due to persecution by gamekeepers, however, they tend to be characteristic of wilder, craggy areas of mountainous forest – a habitat in keeping with their plaintive eerie call, a clear mewing. Although they are fine fliers, using every wind current and thermal to soar, circling for hours on broad, motionless wings, wing tips characteristically up-curved and spread like fingers – they actually spend more of the day perched than on the wing, on trees, or fenceposts or on outstanding rocks.

Buzzards feed chiefly on small ground mammals, particularly rabbits. Frogs and lizards are also taken, as are large insects. Practically all their food is taken by dropping onto it from a perch. When hunting in open country with no suitable perches, the bird may pause and hover, head to wind. Their reliance on rabbits for the major proportion of their food led to a reduction in their numbers with the introduction of myxomatosis to rabbit populations in Britain. However, the situation did not become as bad as many were worried that it might. Breeding success may have been reduced for a few years, but Buzzards are adaptable birds and soon made the switch to alternative prey.

The reduction in breeding success after the introduction of myxomatosis was due to a reduction in the number of adult pairs able to breed, for Buzzards are strongly territorial, and the size of territory is closely adjusted to food availability, varying in successive years even in the same pair of birds. Once the territory is established, the birds perform striking aerial displays, swooping and circling above the breeding site, mewing incessantly. The nest is usually built in a tree, though it may be positioned on a crag or bluff in treeless areas. Both birds take part in building or renovating nests. Each pair usually has a number of nests within its territory, used alternatively in different years. Both sexes take their part in incubation.

For some reason, Buzzards are often regarded with disfavour,

Common Buzzard alighting beside prey (top) and (below) 'mantling' its prey in protective threat.

even amongst ornithologists, as lazy, clumsy, rather uninteresting birds, with little to commend them. Yet they are successful birds, and even if when taking wing their flight is heavy and laboured, when in the air and soaring, they are masters of their element.

Common Buzzard

Plate 10. Rough-legged Buzzard
(Buteo lagopus)

The Rough-legged Buzzard is a large buzzard of northern Europe and North America: a bird of open tundra and mountain sides. It is distinguished from the Common Buzzard (*Buteo buteo*) by being a larger bird with a paler head and neck. The European type has a white chin and white tail with a broad subterminal dark brown bar. The breast is normally dark brown, with flecks and mottles of white, forming a broad, dark chestband across the generally paler belly and upper chest. But its most noticeable feature is the possession of feathered legs: flanks, thighs and lower legs are fully feathered, pale in colour with spots or bars of brown. In America the plumage is very variable, and birds may be seen with almost white heads while others are completely dark.

Unlike the Common Buzzard, which is a bird of woodlands and forests, the Rough-legged Buzzard prefers more open country and adapts its life-style accordingly. It hovers more frequently than the Common Buzzard; indeed it is altogether less laboured in flight, soaring and hovering with great grace and ease. Sometimes it may fly low over the open ground, quartering the terrain like a harrier, to turn into the wind and hover when it spots possible prey. It hunts both from the wing and from a perch on a rock, tree or post. When perched, it has a very erect posture.

Rough-legged Buzzards prey largely upon small mammals, particularly on lemmings in the Arctic. As the weather hardens in their northern breeding haunts and food becomes scarce, they migrate south, following the food supply. The extent and intensity of migration depends on the availability of food. In the winter range, where lemmings are not available, the Buzzard shifts its attentions to mice, voles and small rabbits. All food is taken on the ground, by a short glide from a perch or dropping down from a hover.

During the winter migration south to southern Europe and Asia Minor, and in the New World to the central United States, the birds are very gregarious. In the winter range, mated pairs, which remain together even in the migration flock, often adopt a definite territory which they use constantly. They show a definite preference for marshy areas near water during this winter period, concentrating where suitable prey is abundant.

The birds are less strongly territorial during the breeding season and many features of the breeding behaviour are imposed by the rigours of their Arctic breeding grounds. For instance, displays are not extensive, for there is little time for long drawn out displays in the short Arctic summer. By the same token, unlike other birds of prey, the female, once the eggs are laid and she has begun to incubate, never helps in the hunting; the eggs and young must be closely brooded against the cold. Another adaptation to the conditions in the breeding area is shown in the rapid replacement of the first down of the chicks by the second coat – much earlier than in other buzzards. The nest, on a rock ledge, is made of sticks of dwarf willow or other Arctic plants. It is deep, and the birds line it thickly with sphagnum moss. Each pair has several nests within the breeding area which are used alternately, and the same nests are used for many years, a fact reflected in the ring of bright-green vegetation which develops round the nest where the droppings and castings have enriched the thin Arctic soil.

Rough-legged Buzzard

Plate 11. Broad-winged Hawk
(Buteo platypterus)

The Broad-winged Hawk, one of the American representatives of the buzzard group, is a bird of broad-leaved and mixed forest of eastern North America. Preferring extensive areas of woodland, it is found from central Alberta and Nova Scotia to Texas and Florida. Various subspecies occur in different islands in the West Indies. The mainland race *(Buteo platypterus platypterus)* is migratory, moving south to winter from southern Mexico to Peru and Brazil; all island races are non-migratory.

The Broad-winged Hawk is a stocky little buzzard: dark, greyish-brown above, dull-white below, heavily barred and mottled with dusky brown or rufous. The throat is white with obvious streaks, centrally and on the sides. There is a further blackish streak at the corners of the mouth. A distinctive field characteristic is the broad white bar supported by a narrower bar on the tip of the blackish tail. The cere and feet are yellow, the eyes reddish hazel. Females are slightly larger than males.

Like all buzzards, the Broad-wing in the air is a soaring 'hawk' and spends much of its time perched on posts and other vantage points rather than on the wing. It usually hunts from such a perch, more rarely from the air. Broad-winged Hawks feed on small mammals, snakes, frogs, toads and large insects. Most birds can outfly the hawk, although some individuals specialise

in taking nestlings in the season. Crustacea – such as crayfish – and other arthropods are also taken occasionally. Small mammals are swallowed whole, but larger ones, snakes and frogs are skinned before being eaten; insects are swallowed whole or held in the foot and eaten on the wing. Snakes are a particularly favoured food, and aggregations of frogs and toads in the spawning season attract the hawks to swampier areas.

The nest is built in a tree, in a crook or, in the case of conifers, at the base of a horizontal branch near the trunk. Both birds take part in the construction, which may take about three or four weeks to complete. Despite this, the nest is rather small and poorly built. The hawks do not seem to nest in the same restricted area year after year, as do many buzzards, and do not use the same nest more than once. Courtship flights consist of the pair soaring together in small circles, calling with the characteristic, wailing 'su-eee-oh'. Two or three eggs are laid in the nest on a lining of bark chips, and both sexes are believed to share in the incubation and care of the young, which leave the nest at about six weeks.

The migratory, mainland race is gregarious on passage, and may be seen in loose, wheeling flocks of many hundreds as they follow mountain ridges southwards.

Broad-winged Hawk preparing to land.

Broad—winged Hawk

Plate 12. Red-tailed Hawk
(Buteo jamaicensis)

Another New World *Buteo*, the Red-tailed Hawk is found throughout North America, as far north as there is extensive timber. Over most of its range it is a relatively abundant species, easily distinguished by the characteristic clear chestnut tail. Although a number of subspecies are recognised (largely in terms of geographical distribution), all may be described as dark brown above, with rufous or white feather edgings giving a variegated appearance, and white below with some scattered dark streaks and spots, especially across the lower neck and chest. There is a distinctive black stripe at each corner of the mouth and the chestnut tail, paler on the underside than on the upper surface, has a narrow white tip, supported by a broad black band near the end. Females are characteristically larger than the males. Immatures lack the red tail of the adults. In addition, they are somewhat more mottled with white on the back than are the adults, and more streaked below. The tail in the young birds is grey or grey brown, with six to seven narrow bars of dark grey or black.

Red-tailed Hawks are fairly catholic in their choice of habitat and may be found anywhere from deserts at the one extreme to forested land at the other. For the most part, however, they prefer mixed country of open pasture or field with small bluffs and woodlands. Towards the southern edge of their distribution in Mexico and Central America, they are restricted to montane forests of pine or oak. In the colder parts of their range Red-tails are migratory, and northern birds may winter as far south as the Gulf Coast. Powerful and aggressive hawks, they are opportunistic feeders, taking a variety of ground-living prey.

Red-tailed Hawks are territorial throughout the year (although migratory birds may sometimes be encountered in groups). The range of a nesting pair varies from a third of a square mile to about two-and-a-half square miles. They roost as a pair in thick conifers within the territory, taking a warm-up flight of perhaps an hour each morning before starting to hunt. Two to three hours a day are spent on a high perch; the rest of the time the hawks are actively hunting. The diet is extremely varied, but small rodents and rabbits are the mainstay. Lizards and snakes (including rattlesnakes) are also regularly taken, and where gamebirds are abundant, these may form a large proportion of the food in the breeding season. Individuals become specialists: in some areas Red-tails feed almost exclusively on mice in winter; others may concentrate on insects such as grasshoppers and large crickets. The birds may hunt on the wing, gliding low over the ground and seizing their prey, or, as frequently, they hunt from a perch, watching from a high vantage point in a tall tree to swoop down on possible victims. Even adult hawks are unsuccessful in a high proportion of strikes – indeed, far more often than they are successful.

At the beginning of the breeding season the pair soar about above the territory, screaming in the characteristic, hoarse, rasping 'tsee-eeee-arrr', the male often a little behind and above the female. Occasionally, the male may stoop down on the female, who rolls on her back to present her talons. These flights may occur at any time of year but become more regular in the nesting season. Territorial boundary fights become more common too, and may involve all four birds of two conflicting pairs. Large nests of twigs are built in commanding positions, on rock ledges or bluffs, or in trees in an open situation. The same nest may be used year after year. When the site has been selected both birds bring material to repair an old nest or build anew, and they continue to bring green twigs to add to the fabric of the nest throughout the season. Once the nest is complete the female may remain near it or on it for many weeks before laying one to three eggs. Both sexes incubate, although the female, fed by her mate, does the larger share. If food is short, she may have to hunt for herself and hatching success may be reduced.

The eggs hatch in about thirty days, and the chicks remain in the nest for a further forty-five days. While they are in the nest the parents bring food – often more than the young can eat – and remove unwanted food and refuse from the nest site. Once the young are fledged, the nest may still be used as a feeding platform, although the adults feed the fledglings less often, and by this stage do not clear the refuse from the nest. The young hawks are usually independent by about a hundred days. One curiosity of the breeding cycle is that nests are not infrequently shared with Horned Owls. This species, which nests earlier in the year, may appropriate a Red-tail nest; the hawks are forced to nest elsewhere, but may return to the old nest in later years.

Red-tailed Hawk feeding on a wild duck.

Red-tailed Hawk

Plate 13. Goshawk (Accipiter gentilis)

A trained Goshawk on the fist.

The Goshawk is the largest of the true hawks and displays all the type characters of the group, with short, rounded wings and a long, flexible tail enabling it to fly rapidly yet manoeuvre skilfully in dense cover. As in all hawks, there is a marked dimorphism between the sexes. Females are noticeably larger than males and browner in general colouration. They are birds of the northern hemisphere, ranging from the timberline in Alaska, south to California in America and from Scandinavia and Siberia south to Iran, Tibet, Sardinia and Japan in the Old World. Old and New World Goshawks are rather dissimilar and it has been suggested by some authorities that they may be different species.

The European Goshawk (in this picture) is a large, apparently pale-coloured hawk. In fact, the upper parts are slatey brown, and it is only the sides of the head, the eyebrows and chin, together with the breast and belly which are white, heavily streaked and barred with brown. Females, as in all hawks, are more heavily barred and and have a generally browner appearance.

Like all hawks they are birds of woodland, and Goshawks are equally at home in either deciduous or coniferous forests. They are fierce and aggressive hunters, persistent in pursuit of prey – a persistence which, together with the size of prey they can take, and their manoeuvrability and control in dense woodland has made them a popular hawk for sporting falconers (or 'austringers', as those who fly hawks rather than falcons are properly called). They are, however, regarded as difficult hawks to train. In their natural environment, they prey upon large and medium-sized birds and mammals, to the size of grouse or pheasant, and rabbits or hares. In some areas, crows are one of their most important food items. Individuals may specialise in the hunting of particular prey species. A Swedish biologist has recorded that one male Goshawk brought almost exclusively Woodpigeons and Black-headed Gulls back to the nest, while at another nest, only a mile away, Jays were the major prey. Other birds specialise in tree squirrels, pursuing them from branch to branch in the trees, screaming.

Prey is killed by gripping the victim in one foot; as the hawk increases the pressure it draws back its head to escape the flailings of its victim's death throes. The prey is then carefully plucked before being eaten, generally on the ground.

Goshawk pairs remain together as long as both survive. They may separate for the winter, but in early spring the female moves to her nesting place of the previous year, and screams to attract her mate. The pair may then use the nest of the year before, or build a new one. Curiously, if it is a new nest that is to be built, the male seems to do the majority of the work, while if an old nest is repaired, the female takes on the job. As soon as nest building or repair begins, the pair roost together, and just before dawn, the air is torn by a screaming duet from the two birds before they leave the roost.

Incubation begins, as with many raptors, soon after the laying of the first egg. It has been suggested, however, that for the first fifteen days or so of incubation, temperatures under the female are not sufficient to start development of the embryos, and that of the forty odd days between the laying of the first egg and the hatching of the young, only the last twenty-five days or so are effective. (Temperature recordings have been made from below an incubating female using thermocouples.) Perhaps as a result of this, despite the fact that the female starts to sit straight after the laying of the first egg, which in other species of raptors results in the young hatching over a protracted period so that a nest will contain young of a variety of different ages at any one time, in Goshawks the young all seem to hatch more or less simultaneously.

North American Goshawks tend to be migratory, moving south in the autumn along the mountain ridges, following the failing food supplies and circling back north again in the following spring. In Europe the species is more sedentary. The Goshawk's status in Britain is unclear. It certainly existed as a natural species in historical time, but it is probable that most modern birds have established themselves as escapes from falconers, rather than deriving from a persistent small nucleus of the original population.

Goshawk

Plate 14. European Sparrowhawk (Accipiter nisus)

The European Sparrowhawk is another woodland hawk occurring in Europe, the Middle East, North Africa, Asia and northern India. Northern races tend to be migratory, wintering in the southern parts of the breeding range. The male (shown opposite) has slate-grey upper parts, with a dark slate head, rufous cheeks, and chin and throat white or buff, with dark streaks. The rest of the underparts are rufous or white, closely and narrowly barred with dark brown. The tail is slatey-brown with a white tip and a dark subterminal band. There are four or five other bands across the tail but these are not pronounced. The larger female is a much browner bird, with only a tinge of slate. She keeps the buff face and underparts, but has darker and much heavier bars on the plumage, and looks not unlike a small Goshawk.

Sparrowhawks are unobtrusive birds of woodlands and forests, spending much of their time perched in cover. Outside the breeding season, they become more generally distributed, and move out into more open areas, often far from the nearest trees. They will then colonise any terrain as long as it is not absolutely featureless, but offers some relief – hedges, shrubs, or some physical feature – which will provide concealment for hunting. Their method of hunting relies on concealment and surprise. They may watch from a secluded vantage point and then glide down low and silently onto their chosen victim, taking advantage of any irregularity of terrain which will give them the element of surprise. Alternatively they may fly along hedgerows, slipping silently from side to side low over the hedge itself, along woodland edges or stream banks, ready to snatch any bird that panics and breaks cover. They are masters of the use of even the smallest piece of cover, approaching low behind it and flicking over the top at the last minute in a short dash.

Sparrowhawks prey largely on small birds – in Europe sparrows and finches are indeed their commonest prey. After it has killed, the hawk usually carries its prey to a woodland stump or other favoured spot for plucking. (Larger prey may be plucked where they are killed.) Thick horizontal branches, exposed roots or hummocks may also be used as feeding platforms, and the presence of Sparrowhawks within an area is frequently revealed by the discovery of such plucking posts, with around them the remains of old prey – a scattering of feathers and bones.

Unless disturbed by man, breeding populations of Sparrowhawks show great stability, and each breeding site will normally be used over many years by a succession of birds. A new nest is built each year, near the nests of previous years, and a regular site can be recognised by these groups of nests, which persist for many years. The nest is flattish, up to twenty-four inches across, with a deep central cup. The nests are built of twigs by the female; the male may bring material but does not help in the building. Nest-building may start two months before laying, and the birds continue to bring material to the nest during incubation and after hatching. Thus, as the young grow, the central cup of the nest is gradually filled in until the whole structure forms a huge platform on which the young can exercise freely.

Soaring displays occur in most months, but there are other nuptial displays confined to the breeding season. A single hawk or the pair together may fly to and fro over the nest area, with a strangely deliberate, artificially slow wing beat. The hen may spiral up, again on slow wing beats, to about two hundred feet, and plunge into a long dive, with wings closed, to swing up again, still with her wings closed, just before reaching the trees. The birds are not strictly territorial, and do not restrict their hunting activities to the area immediately round the nest; nor do they defend clearly defined boundaries.

The hen incubates the eggs, and is fed all this time by the male. He rarely visits the nest, but tends to call the female off the nest to collect the food he has brought for her and for the chicks. When the young are still small, the mother tears small morsels of flesh from the prey to feed them, and swallows any remains and pellets herself to keep the nest clean. By the twenty-first day, the young can feed themselves and the hen no longer dismembers carcases for them. From this time, she no longer bothers to keep the nest remains of prey. When the young are fledged, the female teaches them to fly and hunt through cover, allowing them to chase her among the trees before dropping the food she has brought for them.

Over most of their range, Sparrowhawks were once extremely common. However, numbers have declined over much of Europe since the 1950s due to widespread use of persistent pesticides, like DDT and Dieldrin. Fortunately, a voluntary ban is now in effect and in places Sparrowhawks are returning to their former abundance.

Cock European Sparrowhawk on 'plucking post'.

European Sparrowhawk

Plate 15. Sharp-shinned Hawk
(Accipiter striatus)

Closely-related to the European Sparrowhawk *(Accipiter nisus)*, and very similar in habit, the Sharp-shinned Hawk is a small accipiter of woodland, with the typical graceful manoeuvrability of the true hawks and an ability to thread its way through dense understorey with ease and speed. Adults are blue-grey above, with a darker, slate crown, a white or buff throat with dark streaks, and rufous or tawny-buff underparts, mottled and barred with white. The tail is white-tipped and has three darker grey bars. The larger female is slightly duskier, with less of the hint of blue on the upper parts, and while in the male the tail is slightly forked or square, in the female it is never forked, but rather square to slightly rounded.

Sharp-shinned Hawks are found in woodlands of both North and South America. In North America they breed north to the limit of the trees, south to South Carolina, and Alabama in the east, and to Nicaragua in the west; in the south-western United States the species is restricted to mountain forests. Curiously, it does not breed in Costa Rica or Panama, but reappears – again in montane forests – in the Andes; through Brazil, Uruguay, Paraguay and northern Argentina it once again becomes more widespread and returns to lowland country. The North American race *(Accipiter striatus velox)* is quite migratory, with birds moving south to winter in the central United States to Costa Rica.

Sharp-shins feed almost entirely on small song birds, which are quite well-plucked before being eaten. (Like the European Sparrowhawk, each bird has a number of favoured plucking posts within its range, to which it returns with prey.) Small mammals, lizards and insects are also taken occasionally. The hunting technique is typical of all woodland accipiters: prey is surprised and taken in a short dash, as the hawk threads easily between the closest of trees. On migration Sharp-shins often follow the course of song birds that are migrating at the same time, harrying these passerine migrants continuously. Females seem to have a greater capacity for food than the smaller males; it is reported that a female can readily eat three small birds one after the other.

When nesting, the hawks withdraw to a dense thicket of trees – particularly favouring coniferous blocks. The nest is built in a crotch, or on a low branch close to the trunk of the tree; occasionally an old crows' nest or squirrels' drey may be appropriated. The nest is lined with small twigs and chips of bark. Both sexes incubate the clutch of four or five eggs, which hatch more or less together. As in the European Sparrowhawk, while both parents may hunt for the young, the male rarely visits the nest once the chicks are hatched, and never feeds the young, more usually calling the female off the nest to pass over the prey from a perch.

Sharp-shinned Hawk

Plate 16. Hen Harrier/Marsh Hawk (Circus cyaneus)

Harriers are medium-sized slender hawks with long narrow wings and a disproportionately long tail giving them a very characteristic silhouette in flight. When hunting, all harriers quarter the ground, flying low, no more than ten feet or so above the vegetation, with a few wing beats followed by a short glide on stiff wings raised above the back in a shallow V.

The Hen Harrier, or Marsh Hawk, is perhaps the most agile of all the harriers. The male is ash-grey with a distinctive white patch at the base of the tail, and black flight feathers tinged with grey at the very tip. The narrow tail has dark bars on the outer feathers which are absent on the centre two. The female, a much larger bird, is a dark brown, heavily streaked hawk, sharing with the male the white rump and barred tail. Both sexes have a distinct facial ruff of short, curly feathers, covering unusually large ear openings (which are probably an adaptation to enable them to hear their prey in long grass). Hen Harriers breed in North America, Europe and Asia, migrating south in winter to reach Korea, Japan, China, India, the Mediterranean and Central America. They are birds of moorland, coastal marsh or open prairies. In North America, they tend to frequent marshland areas more than elsewhere in their range, doubtless because in America there is no competition for this particular habitat with other harriers such as the Marsh Harrier *(Circus aeruginosus)*. For this reason, the Hen Harrier in America is usually given the alternative name of Marsh Hawk. With their characteristic style of flying low over the ground, methodically searching for prey, the majority of prey are taken on the ground by a pounce or grab. Thus, like other harriers, it feeds on small mammals, frogs and insects. However, the Marsh Hawk, being more agile on the wing, can also take flying prey and thus tends to specialise in feeding on adult songbirds – taking them in one foot as they start to rise off the ground in a fine cricketing catch. Although they tend to fly low over the ground when hunting, Marsh Hawks are capable of high soaring flights as effortless as those of buzzards or eagles. Most of them regularly soar at three hundred feet or more when displaying in the spring. Early in the season, the males also perform a striking display flight of dives and upward swoops, plunging down from sixty feet or so to ten feet or less before swooping up again, nearly stalling at the apex of the climb.

Marsh Hawks are birds of open country. They shun woodland because their long wings and method of hunting with measured searching flight do not equip them for hunting amongst trees. As a result, it is not surprising that they almost invariably both roost and nest on the ground. The nest is little more than a flattened mass of reeds and coarse grasses in tall vegetation. The female incubates alone, while the male brings food to her as she sits. He never visits the nest but calls the female off it, and gives her the prey in a spectacular aerial pass.

A remarkable feature in this context is that Marsh Hawks tend to be strongly polygamous, a situation which occurs most often where there is a high density of nesting birds. It is remarkably developed in Orkney where in recent years the sex ratio has been consistently two females to one male, with, each year, some males attending up to six females concurrently. This polygamy has been noted elsewhere in their range and is particularly strange in that it occurs in a species where the female does not normally hunt while incubating, and the male provides all the food. The obvious result is that some females are not supplied with any, or at least not with sufficient food by the cock and must leave the nest to hunt for themselves. This may affect breeding success to a degree – both hatching and brooding success are lower when two females share a male than with monogamous pairs. Strangely, it is higher again with four females, possibly because only older and more experienced males would take on as many as four females, while the bigamists may include younger and less experienced males. Such polygamy is unique amongst birds of prey anywhere, although other harriers and some falcons may occasionally be bigamous.

Not only are Marsh Hawks polygamous; outside the breeding season they tend to roost communally, too, often in groups of ten or more. This tendency is more marked in America, where roosts may be shared with Short-eared Owls *(Asio flammeus)*.

Wash drawing by Donald Watson of the food pass of the Hen Harrier, or Marsh Hawk. Top left: male about to drop prey to female; centre: the female catching the prey, dropped by the male (two methods); bottom: male moving away, the female having caught the prey.

Hen Harrier/Marsh Hawk

Plate 17. Montagu's Harrier (Circus pygargus)

Montagu's Harrier is the most slender of all the harriers. Although the female is very hard to. distinguish from other female grey harriers such as the Marsh Hawk *(Circus cyaneus)*, since all have the same dark-brown, streaky plumage and the same white rump patch, the male can be easily recognised from the black bars on the wings – above and below, and by the chestnut spots on the flanks and under the wings. Like the Marsh Hawk, Montagu's Harrier is a migrant, breeding from Great Britain eastwards through central Europe and central Russia, and wintering in the Mediterranean, in East Africa, and in India and Ceylon. Again, in its breeding quarters it tends to be a bird of fens and marshes and open moorland. However, it is a conservative bird, sticking closely to areas and habitats similar to those of its own birth. As a result, it has weathered the encroachment of its favoured areas by young conifers – self-sown or planted – and has indeed conceived a liking for young conifer stands, and, so to speak, added them to its habitat list. Afforestation schemes in various countries have thus extended the breeding range of this species in recent years.

Although Montagu's Harriers share much of their range with other harriers – both Marsh Hawk *(Circus cyaneus)* and Marsh Harrier *(Circus aeruginosus)* – differences in size and structure reflected in different hunting abilities and thus prey choice, reduce the degree of competition that might otherwise be experienced. Marsh Harriers – heavier birds with the largest and most powerful feet of all the harriers – exploit heavier and less active prey.

Smaller-footed Marsh Hawks are more agile on the wing and are particularly good at catching adult passerine birds. Montagu's Harrier, with the weakest grip of them all – indeed so weak that it is quite common for prey to escape from its clutches – relies on young passerines and insects, lizards, frogs and even snakes.

Montagu's Harriers roost on the ground in a grass 'form' or on a mound. They roost communally, showing an even stronger tendency to do this than other harriers, particularly at the end of the breeding season and before migration. Like all harriers, they also nest on the ground; the nest is a flat mat of reeds, sedges and coarse grass, and while it is built on the ground it is usually surrounded by high vegetation (often young conifers or tall sedges). The female incubates alone; the male brings food to her but does not visit the nest. Instead he calls her off the nest and she takes the prey from him in the air, rolling over on her back to receive it in the typical harrier food-pass. Where the harriers are numerous, they show a strong tendency towards gregarious breeding. During display, several males may collect and display to one female, and it is common to find several nests in one marsh, only a short distance from each other. Bigamy is not unknown.

Montagu's Harrier has the distinction of being probably the rarest British bird of prey. The population of Montagu's Harriers in 1957 was estimated at forty to fifty nesting pairs. In 1973 and 1974 there was no evidence of any pairs breeding at all, although nesting was reported again in 1976.

Montagus Harrier

Plate 18. Marsh Harrier (Circus aeruginosus)

The Marsh Harrier, or Swamp Hawk, occurs in swamps, marshes and open flood plains over almost the whole of the Old World: throughout Europe, Asia, Africa, Australia and elsewhere. In America, where it is absent, its favoured habitat is taken over by the Hen Harrier or Marsh Hawk *(Circus cyaneus)*; in the same way, in Australia, New Zealand and various islands of the Indian Ocean, where the Swamp Hawk is the only harrier and not in competition with any other, it does not confine itself to wet areas, but is also found in open grassland and moorland.

Marsh Harriers are relatively heavily built for harriers. Males have a cream to rusty-buff head, streaked with dark brown. The mantle and back are dark brown or blackish; wing coverts are also dark brown, but when the wings are spread they reveal silvery-grey flight feathers, barred with brown and ending in black tips visible even when the wings are folded. The tail is the same silvery-grey, with a brownish tinge, unbarred beneath. The rest of the underparts are deep chestnut tinged with dark brown. The female, though larger, is generally much more like the male than in many harriers, though essentially browner.

Marsh Harriers spend a great deal of the day on the wing, perching less frequently than other harriers and flying higher over the longer marshland vegetation, at some fifteen to twenty feet. Though they are heavier birds with broader, less steeply angled wings, they still present the normal harrier silhouette, and have the usual harrier habit of gliding with wings held above the back in a stiff V. They feed chiefly on frogs in marshy areas and snakes, lizards and small mammals up to the size of a water vole. They will also take eggs and nestlings of marsh-breeding water fowl, as well as sick or injured adults, coots and duck.

The breeding territory of an individual pair is not large, and in some areas several pairs may breed close together. As in Montagu's Harrier *(Circus pygargus)* several males may join together in displaying to females, but even a solitary male's display is more spectacular than that of other harriers. He may soar high in the air, then plunge two hundred feet or more, twisting and somersaulting, even looping the loop in the rapid descent before swooping up once more to start again. Such displays continue for many hours, and are accompanied by much calling – a shrill "kwee-ah".

The nest is built on the ground in swampy areas almost entirely

Top left: drawing by Eric Ennion of a Marsh Harrier attacking prey. Above: female Marsh Harrier feeding young.

by the female, who pulls up material in her beak before transferring it to her feet to return with it to the nest site. The male sometimes also brings material to the nest, and may often construct a number of false nests in the vicinity. The same general area is used year after year by a pair of birds; even the more northerly individuals which migrate south in winter, return faithfully to their established breeding sites the following season. The female alone sits on the clutch of four or five eggs; she may call loudly for food while she is incubating, and when the male does bring her prey, flies up to take it in the typical harrier 'aerial pass'.

Though once widespread, Marsh Harriers stopped breeding regularly in Britain nearly a hundred years ago, probably as a result of the draining of the fens. They returned to Norfolk in the 1920s and slowly began to spread once more. Tragically, this attempt at recolonisation was thwarted when the birds – at that time numbering perhaps twenty pairs – were hit by the effects of widespread use of pesticides in the 1950s. Now, only one or two pairs breed in closely guarded reserves.

Marsh Harrier

Plate 19. Gyrfalcon (Falco rusticolus)

Wood engraving of a Gyrfalcon by Thomas Bewick.

The remaining birds in this part of the book belong to the genus *Falco*, the true falcons. Falcons characteristically take their prey on the wing, by 'stooping' upon it in a rapid dive, or by straight pursuit. Towards this end they have torpedo-shaped bodies and long, pointed wings. The bill is short and powerful with a distinct 'tooth' on each side of the upper mandible, which fits into a notch in the lower beak. The legs are short and the feet very powerful, for many falcons kill their prey by striking them with the talons while still in the air.

The largest and most magnificent of the falcons is the Gyrfalcon, a bird of the Arctic, of the barren tundras and mountains of Arctic Europe, Greenland and Iceland, of Asia and North America. Most Gyrfalcons are resident, although some, particularly young birds, migrate southwards in winter, and even residents may leave the breeding territory and move to open sea coasts where food is more available.

Gyrfalcons occur in a variety of different colour phases. In the dark phase, shown here, the upper parts are dark-slate coloured, with close, brown bars; the tail is tipped with white. The crown and sides of the head are dark brown, streaked with white. The forehead, in marked contrast, is white with shafts of black. Chin, throat and upper breast are white, with small, pear-shaped dark spots; the lower breast and belly are white with larger spots. Falcons show sexual dimorphism, and females are larger and darker than males. In its light phase the Gyrfalcon gives the impression of being almost pure white; the whole body plumage is clear white, usually streaked on the crown, and spotted and barred grey or brown elsewhere. The tail is white, still barred with brown, and the wings are white, barred grey-brown and with black tips.

Between these two phases are a whole host of intermediates, so many in fact that, in the past, Gyrfalcons were divided into a number of distinct subspecies: *Falco rusticolus rusticolus* in northern Europe and Asia, *F. r. intermedius* in the Urals and *F. r. uralensis* in north Siberia. The race in north-eastern Canada – an almost pure white form – was dubbed *F. r. obsoletus*, while Iceland and Greenland had their own subspecies too – *F. r. islandicus* and *F. r. candicans*. However, there is a great deal of variation in colour even within these groups and it is probable that the separation of each race into distinct subspecies is unjustified. As a general rule, though, it may be noted that the more northerly birds tend to be paler, while at the southern extremes of the range, the birds tend to be darker.

Gyrfalcons breed on rock ledges or on a crag – typically in a gorge or a river valley. They build no nest, but merely make a scrape in the ledge. The site chosen is usually well overhung to protect the eggs and young from late snow. A characteristic feature of such a site is the mass of droppings, pellets and food scraps which accumulate below – decomposition is not rapid in the Arctic. The display is short, and includes swoops and dives, with the female turning on her back to present claws, as in other accipiters. The female alone incubates and rarely leaves the nest – the short display and the close incubation reflecting, as in the Rough-legged Buzzard (*Buteo lagopus*), the short, cold Arctic summer. Gyrs do not seem to breed every year; traditional breeding sites are unoccupied for about fifty percent of all years, and since the birds are very faithful to their nest sites, it seems likely that they breed only in alternate years.

Gyrfalcons prey chiefly on birds, especially Arctic ptarmigan and grouse. In many areas, breeding success seems to rely almost entirely on the abundance of these game birds which may make up ninety percent by weight of all the food. Mammals form by comparison a very small proportion of the food and it is not surprising to find that breeding success is not related to cycles or numbers of lemmings in the Arctic, but is markedly influenced by fluctuations in ptarmigan populations. In winter, on the sea coasts, many sea birds are also preyed upon, up to the size of large ducks and even geese. Gyrfalcon kills can often be recognised by a clear notch in the breastbone of the prey – it may even be completely split in two.

When hunting, the Gyrfalcon flies fast and low, catching its prey by direct pursuit rather than 'stooping' as other falcons. They seem less able to fly in warmer climates. Fast flying involves great muscular activity and produces a great deal of internal heat. Birds have a comparatively low lethal temperature, and it is therefore possible that while rapid flight is possible in the chill of the Arctic, in warmer temperatures only considerably less intense muscular activity can be accommodated without raising the birds' temperature above its lethal limit. Although Gyrfalcons have been manned for falconry, this fact, together with their reluctance to stoop, or to 'wait on' (hovering above the head of the falconer while the prey is flushed) has made them less popular than other large falcons.

Gyrfalcon

Plate 20. Duck Hawk (Falco peregrinus)

If one falcon above all excites fanaticism amongst its admirers it is the Duck Hawk (or Peregrine, as it is called in Europe). It is an aggressive, fearless bird, a superb flier with a complete and easy mastery of the air. Characteristic of rocky areas, both inland and on the coast, the Duck Hawk is found throughout the world, some eighteen different races being described from different areas, breeding in all the major continents and in many island groups. They are medium-sized falcons, with stocky bodies, short tails and sharply-pointed, long wings. The primary wing feathers are long and slender for speed in flight, the inner, secondaries, are broad to give strength for lifting heavy prey. The adult male, referred to by falconers as the *tiercel,* has a blue-grey back, barred darker grey. The head is dark-slate, with the crown, nape and back of the neck, bluish-slate; the area round the eyes and ear coverts is black with cheeks and chin white or buff and a pronounced broad, black moustachial stripe. The upper breast is white or buff with black spots, and the rest of the underparts are darker and closely barred. The tail is the same slate grey as the upper parts, barred blackish towards the end, and tipped with white. The larger female, or *falcon,* is very like the male but darker on the lower back and rump and much more heavily barred. Immature birds, as the female shown here, have the slate feathers tipped with brown, giving overall a brownish tinge.

But whatever its characteristics, in the air the Duck Hawk is unmistakable. Its stocky form always seems somehow smoother and cleaner in outline than that of other falcons. Its speed is breathtaking and its skill and manoeuvrability masterful. In normal flight the Duck Hawk flicks along cliff edges or bluffs with short, rapid wingbeats, five or six to a second, interspersed with short glides. When hunting, it emerges as the fastest bird on earth, both in straight pursuit, and in 'stooping' down on its prey from above. All falcons characteristically pursue their prey on the wing, either in straight chase or by 'stooping', but the Duck Hawk uses both techniques, pursuing smaller prey and killing them by gripping them in the talons, 'stooping' down on larger prey from above and commonly striking them dead in mid-air with the long hind 'killing' toe.

'Stooping' is a way of increasing the speed with which the falcon makes contact with its prey. A Duck Hawk in full 'stoop' reaches a speed variously estimated as between a hundred and fifty and two hundred miles per hour. The momentum produced adds weight to the bird and enables it to kill birds twice as heavy as itself.

Duck Hawks feed on prey taken exclusively on the wing, chiefly large birds such as gamebirds – particularly favoured are Red Grouse and Woodpigeons. Where the birds frequent the coast, they may also take duck, small geese, gulls and waders. When the falcon has killed, it plucks the feathers from its prey before beginning to eat. The amount of plucking varies with individuals: some pluck the prey very thoroughly, while others pull out only a few feathers. The prey may be eaten where it falls, but smaller kills are often carried to favoured feeding sites.

Female Duck Hawk in typical stooping flight.

A pair of Duck Hawks mate for life and seem very attached to each other. They are often seen together, roosting or resting in rocks or trees, or circling above their range. In the breeding season, the male takes up position near a suitable ledge, and flies out to attract the female to the site. Once the site is decided upon, male and female perform spectacular display flights. The male may dive at the female, or vice versa, and the pair tumble over one another in the air – but all this at incredible speed and with split-second accuracy. The male will also feed the female during courtship in a ceremony in which he bows up and down with a chittering call; food is also passed in the air. While the Duck Hawk is usually a silent bird away from the nest, at the nest site it is incredibly noisy with a very varied vocabulary: the chittering mentioned above, together with a 'hek-hek-heking' at intruders and a shrill screaming cry "shreeeeee!". There is no nest: the eggs are laid in a scrape in the earth, or the nest of a buzzard, raven or eagle may be appropriated. The birds occasionally nest in buildings. The female does most of the incubation, but the male also takes a share and develops a true brood-patch. The tiercel also hunts for both himself and his mate, bringing food to the nest, or passing it to the female in flight. Both birds are very aggressive at the nest, and will attack any intruder, regardless of size.

Because of its speed, its grace, its spectacular stoops and the comparatively large size of the prey it can take, the Duck Hawk has always been in great demand by falconers. It is *the* falcon; for centuries it was reserved only for the use of nobles and kings. Many modern falconers are now rearing these birds to release them and re-establish them in the wild, for in both Britain and America populations have been hard hit by the poisons of persistent pesticides.

Duck Hawk

Plate 21. Hobby (Falco subbuteo)

Hobby stalling to alight on perch.

A slim, long-winged, long-tailed falcon of about the same size as a European Kestrel and looking very much like a diminutive Duck Hawk, the Hobby is a bird of rather open country with a distribution extending over the whole of the Palearctic region. It breeds from Britain right the way across Europe into Russia, but is essentially a summer visitor only, migrating in the winter to Africa, north India and China. Hobbies may be distinguished from Duck Hawks *(Falco peregrinus)* by their much smaller size, by the fact that the moustachial stripe is narrower and that the bluff underparts are marked with vertical streaks rather than horizontal bars. Most distinctive, however, is the fact that the lower belly and thighs are a clear chestnut. As in Duck Hawks, the female is rather browner than the male and more streaked.

Hobbies are very swift and graceful fliers – in flight the long, slender wings are extraordinarily flexible and the movements appear very leisurely. But the speed is deceptive, for the Hobby is fast enough to take swifts and swallows on the wing. Prey includes insects as well as small birds, and all food is taken in flight with a distinctive hunting technique absolutely characteristic of the Hobby. When taking small birds, the falcon dashes into the middle of a flock seizing one of the birds in passing; when feeding on insects it passes and repasses through swarms taking the prey in its claws and passing it to the beak with one foot while still in flight. Insects are eaten on the wing, as may be smaller birds. Larger kills are taken to a suitable feeding site on a tree branch or on the ground, to be plucked and eaten. Although Hobbies have no difficulty in taking larger prey, when insects are abundant they tend to form the bulk of their food, particularly in late summer in their breeding haunts, and in the winter quarters. (The falcons' arrival in their wintering areas coincides with the start of the rainy season in these countries – which means a constant supply of insect food.)

In its breeding haunts, the Hobby frequents mostly open country with scattered woodland. It avoids dense forest or very open areas even in the winter quarters where it takes to savannah and open bush. On migration, and to some extent in the wintering grounds, they are fairly gregarious birds, often roosting and feeding in company. Flocks numbering many hundreds may pass on migration together. They are always playful falcons and aerobatic displays may be seen at any time as if just through sheer high spirits. But their grace and skill in flight is shown to perfection in courtship, when the pair tumble together in the air, stooping, looping the loop, rolling and gliding upside down – all at breakneck speed. The pair may soar high over the nest site with the male diving down at the female. As with Duck Hawks, the male feeds the female in display, both in an aerial food-pass and from a perch. No nest is built – the pair take over the old nests of other birds, even occasionally displacing the occupier from a new nest. Two or three eggs are laid and again both parents take a part in incubation, though the female's is the larger share.

Hobby

Plate 22. Pigeon Hawk (Falco columbarius)

The Pigeon Hawk, or Merlin, once again is not a true hawk, but a very small falcon, about the size of a large thrush, or small pigeon. They occur over much of the northern hemisphere, breeding in America north of a line from California to Newfoundland, and in the Old World from northern Britain, through Scandinavia and Russia across to Mongolia. They are partial migrants; American birds winter south to Ecuador and Venezuela while European and Asian birds migrate to North Africa and Arabia, north India, and Indo-China.

Neither sex has the moustachial stripe characteristic of the Duck Hawk *(Falco peregrinus)* or Hobby *(Falco subbuteo)*. The male has light, slaty upper parts which appear distinctly blue and a darker, greyer head finely streaked with black. There is an indistinct white eyebrow above a black stripe through the eye itself, and a narrow, white band across the forehead. Chin and throat are greyish white, while the rest of the underparts are rufous-buff streaked red-brown. The tail is slate-grey above, paler at the tip, conspicuously barred. Females are dark brown with no slate markings, with a more pronounced white forehead and eyebrows and with clear, thin rufous bars on the tail. The underparts are lighter in colour but more heavily streaked and barred than those of the male.

As with all falcons, the size and flight are the most striking characteristics. Pigeon Hawks are small birds of open country: of moorland, short grass steppe, sea shores and dunes. They fly low over the ground, swift and active, with rapidly beating wings and sudden changes of direction. The flight seems almost erratic, like that of a snipe, and energetic, for they glide less between wing beats than do other falcons. They feed chiefly on small ground-living birds – larks, pipits, buntings – taken in short and extremely rapid dashes. The food also includes insects (in North America, Pigeon Hawks prey extensively on dragonflies) and small mammals. Like the Hobby, the Pigeon Hawk eats its insect prey on the wing, pausing in flight to hover while it feeds. The balance of the diet is estimated from one study as eighty percent birds, fifteen percent insects and five percent small mammals – the inclusion of small mammals here emphasising that this is a falcon that takes the majority of its food on or near the ground.

Pigeon Hawks are migratory. Since they are small, and relatively light, they tend to follow sea coasts when on migration to avoid long crossings. They return to the same general breeding areas each spring, although not necessarily to the same actual nest site. They are very catholic in their taste of breeding site. In open country or sparse woodland, they frequently nest in a scrape on the ground in thick vegetation; shore-nesting birds breed amongst the sand dunes and a considerable nest may accumulate as the sitting bird plucks nearby dune grasses and tucks them under itself. Pigeon Hawks may even withdraw to more densely-wooded areas to breed – areas they would normally avoid. Here they will nest in trees, usually taking over the old nests of other species. The female lays five or six eggs – rather a high number for a falcon – and takes the greater part of the incubation. The male may sit occasionally, but plays his major role in hunting for the female, calling her off the nest to receive the prey. After the eggs hatch, he brings food directly to the nest, but it is the female who actually feeds the young.

In the heyday of falconry, Pigeon Hawks were a lady's falcon, being light, delicate birds, and considered easy to train. They were usually flown only for a single season and were then returned to the wild and a fresh bird taken and trained.

Pigeon Hawk

Plate 23. Common Kestrel
(Falco tinnunculus)

In both Europe and America Kestrels are amongst the most abundant and probably the most familiar of all the falcons and yet the least typical of the group. For while most falcons hunt by chasing their prey on the wing in rapid pursuit, or by 'stooping' upon it from above, Kestrels hunt from a low hover. This hunting style is absolutely characteristic. The falcons are usually seen in open country quartering the ground, continually circling to turn into the wind and hover, with broadly-fanned tail and quivering wings, as they search the ground for prey. Such a hunting technique – more like that of a hawk than that of a true falcon – has presumably developed in the Kestrel because these are falcons that have specialised in taking prey on the ground. The strength of the wind determines the mode of hovering. In a flat calm, the bird must maintain its position by flapping its wings quite hard. In strong winds, it scarcely moves its wings at all, and moves from stand to stand with a rapid side-slip. About one in eight hovers results in a 'stoop' to the ground to seize prey. It is not a fast 'stoop' like that of a Duck Hawk or Hobby, but more a settling onto the ground, wings held arched above the back ready to take off again.

Hen Common Kestrel returning to nest with a fieldmouse.

The Kestrel feeds largely on small rodents caught in short grass. They will also take small birds, lizards and snakes, frogs and insects – almost anything that may be taken on the ground.

The Common Kestrel, shown here, is a small, highly coloured falcon, found throughout Europe, Asia and Africa. (In America, their place is taken by the American Kestrel, *Falco sparverius*.) They are reddish-brown birds with long wings and long, broad tails, characteristic of open fields, grasslands and moorland. Males have a blue-grey head and lower back with a bright chestnut mantle, sometimes marked with small black spots. The chestnut continues over the upper parts of the wings, although the primary flight feathers are clear black. The tail is slate, tipped greyish-white, with a broad, black bar below the tip, and a varying number of narrow bars above, though these may be entirely absent. The sides of the face and the forehead are cream, separated from cream chin and throat by a dark-grey moustachial stripe. The rest of the underparts are buff, spotted with black on the breast, belly and flanks. Female Common Kestrels are also highly-coloured. While the male has a blue-grey head, the female's crown and nape are the same chestnut as the mantle and back. The crown and nape are streaked with black above, but this develops into close and distinct bars lower on the mantle and back. She has a blue-grey rump and a bright chestnut tail tipped with buff, and with a broad subterminal bar of black supported by other narrower, blackish bars above. The female has a cream forehead like that of the male, but lacks a distinct moustache. Underparts are buff or cream, streaked or barred with black more heavily than the male. When not quartering the ground for prey, or in their distinctive hover, Kestrels are frequently seen perched, very upright, on trees, fenceposts, telegraph poles and the like.

Both European and American Kestrels are generally rather solitary birds and pairs are spaced out over a wide area, not usually tolerating others within half a mile or so. They breed on a ledge or a cliff, making a small scrape in the ground or using the old nest of another bird. In recent years the European birds have taken quite regularly to nesting on buildings – on farms, but also in towns. Kestrels are not superb fliers as are other falcons, and the courtship display is not particularly spectacular. The male may soar and circle, diving at the female in a series of short 'stoops'. During this performance, the female usually remains perched in a conspicuous position. The hen Kestrel lays four or five eggs and while incubation may start, as is normal amongst birds of prey, with the first egg, it may also be delayed until the clutch is complete. The male takes little part in incubation, although he may occasionally relieve the female. Instead he brings food to the nest while the female is sitting and the young are quite small. When the young are old enough to break up prey themselves and the female can hunt more, the male is seen less often at the nest.

Gareth Parry. 1975.

Common Kestrel

Plate 24. Lesser Kestrel (Falco naumanni)

The Lesser Kestrel breeds in the countries bordering the Mediterranean and to the east as far as China. It is a migrant, moving to Africa, and, in smaller numbers, to India during the winter.

They are smaller than the Common Kestrel (*Falco tinnunculus*) and of more slender build. Males have a clear, unspotted chestnut back, and bluer head and tail; the underparts are often clear and unstreaked. More striking are the behavioural differences. Lesser Kestrels are highly gregarious birds, both on their breeding grounds and in winter quarters, and are very noisy birds, constantly crying with a plaintive "whee" and a clattering "chet, kee, kee, kee". They frequently hunt in groups – even in quite large parties – quartering the ground as do Common Kestrels, but hovering less often – and, when they do hover, tending to hang poised on still wings, less commonly with rapidly beating wings as the Common Kestrel.

Throughout their range, Lesser Kestrels are birds of open country, grass plains and steppes – even arid semi-desert. They feed largely on insects taken on the ground from a hover, or hawked in mid-air. It is perhaps because of their diet that they can afford to associate in such large hunting groups: indeed, it may be that large parties actually increase hunting success by flushing the insect prey. Insects comprise over eighty percent of the total diet. The birds feed largely on grasshoppers in the breeding range, and, in their winter quarters, on flying termites.

Gregarious throughout the year, Lesser Kestrels nest in colonies, of from two or three pairs to a hundred or more. Colonies of fifteen to twenty pairs are common. They nest in old walls or fortifications, or high on buildings. Natural sites, such as a cliff face with many ledges, are used much less commonly. There is little aerial display: in courtship the male feeds the female with insects or other prey, caught in his foot, and transferred to his bill before being passed to the female. Eggs are laid in a bare, unlined scrape. No nest is made and the clutch of four or five eggs is incubated by the female. All prey is brought by the male, and even after the eggs are hatched when the female may assist in the hunting, the male plays the major role of provider.

Lesser Kestrel

Plate 25. Red-footed Falcon (Falco vespertinus)

The Red-footed Falcon is one of the most unusual of the falcons in a number of respects. It is probably the most gregarious of all the falcons – at all times. Red-footed Falcons breed in large colonies, migrate in huge flocks, and, outside the breeding season, also roost in company. In addition, this falcon is markedly crepuscular, flying mainly at dawn and dusk, and well able to catch prey in very poor light. It hunts from a hover, but is also able to run freely on the ground.

Red-footed Falcons breed in Central Europe and Asia, wintering mainly in Africa. They are very striking birds. The male is completely grey: dark-slate above, darkest – almost black – on the rump and paler grey below. The lower belly and thighs are bright chestnut and there is a red ring of bare skin around the eye. The larger female has a chestnut head with a cream forehead, chin and cheeks. The sides of the head are rufous-grey. She has a bright chestnut, moustachial stripe. Upper parts are grey-brown, heavily barred; chest and breast are buff with dark spots, the lower belly clear, creamy buff. Both sexes have bright red feet – a marked contrast from the usual falcon yellow. In the male these red feet are emphasised by the chestnut 'thighboots'.

Red-footed Falcons fly relatively slowly, and quite low, quartering the ground like kestrels, coming head to the wind to stall and hover to search for prey. They hunt well into the evening, in very poor light, preying on frogs and insects taken largely on the ground. At one breeding colony, nearly seventy-five percent by weight of food items taken was frogs, the remainder being almost entirely insects. In wintering areas, the falcons become almost entirely insectivorous, concentrating on grasshoppers and flying termites,

as do Lesser Kestrels (*Falco naumanni*). The falcons perch frequently on telegraph poles, posts and trees, and also both perch and run freely on the ground in pursuit of prey. Red-footed Falcons favour open country dotted with woodland or copses, hunting over fields and open ground. The main wintering quarters are the savannahs of south Central Africa (winter corresponds here with the rainy season and there is thus an abundance of insects for the falcons to feed upon).

These falcons really are extraordinarily sociable, migrating in flocks of many hundreds together. In winter quarters they roost in enormous gatherings, often numbering between four and five thousand birds together. Individual trees may hold a hundred birds or more. Curiously the roost is often shared with crows. The birds do not share trees, but occupy different areas within the same clump, there being distinct crow trees and falcon trees. The falcons hunt in large parties too, and their gregariousness extends even to their breeding. Red-footed Falcons breed in colonies in the old nests of rooks. In much the same way as the falcons may share a roost with crows, the breeding rookeries are occupied and eggs laid when the rooks are in occupation. The falcons do not eject the resident rooks from their nests but use empty ones within the colony.

Both sexes of falcon share in the incubation and rearing of the young, flying out from the breeding rookery to the open country more characteristic of them to hunt for food. As the young grow and begin to fly, they leave the nest, and move to the edge of the clump of trees in which they were raised, flying out to meet their parents when they return with food.

Red-footed Falcon

THE PLATES

OWLS

Plate 26. Barn Owl (Tyto alba)

The Barn Owl is a widely distributed species, occurring, in a variety of local races, in North and South America, Europe, across to western Russia, Africa, southern Asia and Australia. It is not strictly cosmopolitan in that, with the exception of parts of Europe and the United States it is rarely found outside tropical regions. A medium-sized bird, the Barn Owl has pale to orange buff upper parts, spotted dark-grey or white, a pronounced white facial disc (a concave saucer around the eyes and ears, used to concentrate and focus sounds) and white or buff underparts; there is both a light-breasted and a dark-breasted form. Sexes are more or less alike. Barn Owls have long wings and a buoyant flight; a specialised feather structure on the outer edge of the main flight feathers of the wings makes this flight absolutely silent.

Barn Owls roost during the day singly or in pairs in dark places in ruins, churches, barns or lofts or in hollow trees, standing bolt upright and motionless in a dark corner. They emerge in the early evening to hunt over open ground: heaths, moorlands and open grassland, sweeping backwards and forwards over the ground, with a series of slow flaps alternating with long glides, rarely more than a few feet above the ground. An owl will often follow hedges or ditches, or rough field edges where prey will be more abundant. It catches its prey in flight by suddenly dropping to the ground and gripping its victim in its talons before crushing the head with its bill. It may hover briefly before diving onto its prey, and Barn Owls occasionally hunt from a perch, dropping or gliding onto prey in nearby undergrowth. The food is made up mainly of small nocturnal rodents. Small birds at roost, particularly sparrows, can also form an important part of their diet. The owl swallows its prey whole, only dismembering it if it is too large. Indigestible portions are formed into firm pellets and cast back up to be voided. Barn Owl pellets are characteristically glossy, almost varnished, black in colour, and each bird will cast two oval pellets in every twenty-four hours.

Pairs are assumed to be territorial because local populations tend to be regularly spaced. Little is known of the mating display, but wing-clapping in flight has been noted, and the male has been seen to present food to the female. Any display is accompanied by frequent beak-clicking as the birds snap the upper mandible onto the lower. The owls nest in a hollow tree, or in a dark crevice within an old building, choosing much the same type of site for breeding as for roosting. No nest is built, and the eggs are laid directly onto the flat floor of the nesting hollow. An accumulation of pellets and droppings serves to hold the eggs in place, and the eggs, originally pure white in colour, rapidly become stained till they appear yellow. The female incubates from three to seven eggs, starting after she has laid the first egg; throughout incubation she is fed by the male. There is a very protracted breeding season: Barn Owls may breed between late February and September. This enables many pairs to undertake two broods in a year. The staggered hatching of the young (so that the youngest may die if food is scarce, leaving sufficient food for the survivors) and the extended breeding season are almost certainly adaptations to enable the number of young reared each year to be adjusted precisely to the differing availabilities of food.

The Barn Owl's habit of roosting in dark and derelict spots, of haunting churchyards and old buildings, its silent flight, and white ghostly appearance have combined to surround it with superstition. The eerie reputation is enhanced in that there are many reliable reports of Barn Owls glowing in the dark – presumably because the plumage has picked up luminescent bacteria from decaying wood. The call too is in keeping: a long, eldritch scream. Yet the Barn Owl is in fact extremely beneficial to man. Its habit of roosting in old buildings brings it close to human habitation and activities, and it proves itself an important predator of rats and mice and small grain-eating birds. So much so that until comparatively recently, both British and European farmers used to build special owl doors under the gables of their barns to encourage the owls to use them as roosts and nest sites.

Regrettably, the Barn Owl is now declining in numbers. In 1932 there were estimated to be twenty-five thousand pairs breeding in England and Wales. In a census of 1964 there was found to have been a drastic fall in numbers in many areas, due in part to pesticides, but compounded by the removal of hedges from farmland and the replacement of old barns with newer, open-style buildings.

Previous page: female Barn Owl carrying a short-tailed vole.

Barn Owl

Plate 27. Tawny Owl (Strix aluco)

The Tawny Owl, perhaps the most abundant and most familiar of all the European owls, occurs in woodlands more or less throughout the whole of Europe and Asia. Curiously, its British distribution does not extend to include Ireland. It is a medium-sized owl, easily recognised by its disproportionally large, very rounded head and well-marked facial disc, distinguished from the only other woodland owl of Europe of about the same size, the Long-eared Owl (*Asio otus*) by a stockier build, and lack of ear tufts. The plumage is brown, spotted and streaked with white above and buff below, streaked with dark brown; the ground colour is variable from grey-brown to rufous. The call is perhaps its most familiar feature – one that everyone associates with the owl – the famous, quavering "Hooooo–oooooo. Tuwhit, Who-hooo". Another common call is an excited, strident: "Kee-wick!". Although essentially nocturnal, it is nonetheless quite a regular daytime hunter. Its preferred prey are small rodents – mice and voles – but it has fairly catholic tastes and makes up a fair proportion of its diet from beetles and earthworms. The Tawny Owl hunts by dropping onto likely prey from an observation post; it does not hawk for its prey on the wing as might a Barn Owl. Each owl has its own, especially favoured, hunting perches to which it will return night after night; the ground below becomes splashed with the lime from its droppings. Hunched on top of such a perch, the bird will slowly turn his head from side to side, to and fro, listening intently, for Tawny Owls hunt almost exclusively by sound. A wriggle of the neck, sudden interest in the face as he fixes upon an unsuspecting vole – and he pounces.

These are cosmopolitan birds, not restricted to any one habitat but able to exploit equally well pine forest, deciduous woodland and open arable country. But they are strictly territorial, containing their activities within the clear confines of their own established home range. These territories are hotly defended: each autumn, every boundary resounds to the shrieking and cater-wauling of the owls whose territories it separates, disputing each other's claim to their lands and re-affirming the boundary line. Indeed, these territories have remarkably stable boundaries, which persist year after year – boundaries which outlive the span of individual owls, but are characteristic rather of the territory itself. The reasons for this are many: once a territory has been established, its confines are respected by its neighbours. The owls are long-lived, and once the same territory has been defended for a number of years it becomes almost inviolable. Even if the owner dies, the neighbours will not encroach, and on the owner's death the territory is usually taken over in its entirety by a newcomer rather than annexed to a neighbour's domain. The newcomer enters a territory whose boundaries are already clear, so that the pattern of stable territories is continued.

In many species of birds and mammals, territory size in any one season is closely related to the abundance and availability of food. Amongst Tawny Owls, however, the size of a territory is clearly dictated largely by social factors and thus cannot be closely moulded to prey availability. This situation is further exacerbated by the fact that populations of small rodents – the owls' preferred food – fluctuate widely in numbers, with as much as a five-fold difference in numbers between successive years. Since the Tawny Owl cannot adjust its territory to prey availability, it changes its life-style. Tawny Owls breed only in years of great prey abundance. In lean years they do not even attempt to breed at all. When they do breed, the number of eggs laid and the number of young that survive are closely related to the abundance of food.

In this species the manner of this control can be closely defined, for Tawnies are perhaps the best studied of all the owls. Observations on breeding pairs have been made by persuading the birds to breed in artificial nest boxes, fitted with a mirror so that an observer on the ground can see into the box itself. Even the amount and species of prey brought to the nest can be recorded; a light beam focused across the mouth of the nest box broken by the return of the hunter, triggers by remote control a camera trained on the nest box. The prey item and the time are recorded on film. From such work we know that a female Tawny Owl lays from one to three eggs, normally in a hollow in a rotten trunk or branch. While she incubates the eggs and broods the young owlets, the male steps up his hunting efforts and brings prey to the nest to feed her. However he cannot usually bring sufficient prey every night to sustain her and she makes up for this shortfall by drawing on fat deposits laid down before incubation began. But these fat deposits are only a reserve and, during incubation, most of the female's food must still be provided by the male. If prey abundance is low and he fails to bring sufficient to the nest, the female herself must leave the nest to hunt and the eggs or chicks will chill and die. Thus the breeding success of the owls is tied to prey abundance. If the female cannot build up sufficient fat reserves to sustain her through the breeding attempt she does not start to lay. The next check relates to the male's ability to keep her supplied with food while she is incubating so that she does not have to leave the nest and leave the eggs to chill. Finally, unless he can step up his catch to provide both for the female and the newly-hatched young for the first fifteen days after hatching (while the female is still brooding them) one or more of the young will die all the same. With different degrees of food shortage, the number of chicks that die relate exactly to the amount of food that is available. It is a very fine-tuned system.

Accurate calculations have been made of the energy required by an incubating female and by a female and newly-hatched young. By subtracting the energy value of the female's fat deposits, one can estimate exactly the amount of food which the male must bring to the nest daily for incubation to be successful, as well as the amount he must bring in the next fifteen days if one, two or three chicks are to survive. These predictions are borne out in observations of successful and unsuccessful nests.

Tawny Owl

Plate 28. Long-eared Owl (Asio otus)

Long-eared Owls are distributed in a wide band right around the northern hemisphere between latitudes 30°N and 65°N. They are relatively small owls, about fourteen inches high, and are characterised by having very pronounced 'ear-tufts' (These tufts, sported by many owls, are not true ears, but are merely bunches of feathers sprouted above the facial disc.) The plumage is freckled and mottled buff and grey-brown. Underparts are lighter buff with dark streaks and cross-bars. The facial disc is well-marked, and the eyes are clear yellow. Long-eared Owls are found in light woodland, both broad-leaved and coniferous, and are typical of small copses and isolated clumps of trees amongst agricultural land. They are comparatively sedentary birds, although the most northerly breeders move south or west in winter.

Long-eared Owls are very strongly nocturnal – indeed the most nocturnal owls of the world. While most owls hunt in the late evening and early morning, either side of midnight, Long-eared Owls are really birds of the middle of the night. They hunt along forest edges and hedgerows preying predominantly on voles, mice and rats. Like Barn Owls (*Tyto alba*) they take small birds at roost, and, in addition, may prey on large insects. They spend the day asleep, standing bolt upright, very tall and thin, at the base of tree branches, huddled close against the trunk. Occasionally, outside the breeding season, in autumn and winter, they may be found roosting in small parties of up to eight or ten birds.

Like most owls, Long-eared Owls hunt more by sound than by sight – another reason for having especially noiseless flight in addition to the more obvious one of a silent approach to prey. The ears in owls are arranged near the focal points of the facial disc but positioned slightly asymmetrically. Sounds reaching the bird will ordinarily take longer to reach one ear than the other, and by the time difference between the sound reaching the nearer and further ears, some indication can be derived of the direction from which the sound has come. The asymmetrical positioning of the ears of owls exaggerates this effect and enables them to pinpoint exactly the direction and origin of sounds which reach them.

Long-eared Owls nest in trees in twig nests made and abandoned by other large birds, often taking over a disused crow's nest. Birds of more open, montane areas quite frequently nest on the ground. Breeding success reflects prey abundance to a large extent, from four to five eggs being laid in a normal year and up to eight or ten eggs laid in a peak vole year. Females alone incubate, while males bring prey to the nest.

Long-eared Owls are amongst the most secretive and elusive of all the birds of prey – largely due to an extraordinarily retiring nature. Yet they are probably more abundant today than is generally appreciated.

Long-eared Owl at nest.

Long—eared Owl

Plate 29. Short-eared Owl (*Asio flammeus*)

The Short-eared Owl is capable of extreme movements of the head on the shoulders, compensating for the fixity of its gaze.

The Short-eared Owl is one of the few diurnal owls: a medium-sized bird which hunts both during the day and at dusk over open country. It is a pale brown bird with boldly-streaked underparts, having longish wings, (a fact which reflects its habit of hunting on the wing) marked with a dark patch on the wrist both on the upper and lower surfaces. The owl has short 'ear-tufts', scarcely visible on top of the head, and brilliant yellow eyes, whose hardness is emphasised by a surrounding of dark-tipped feathers in an otherwise pale facial disc.

It is a widely distributed species, breeding throughout the Old and New Worlds between 40°N and 70°N, and extending right down into the southern half of South America. Birds breeding at the northerly extremes of the range are migratory, moving to more central or southerly parts of the range during the winter. Over most of its range, the Short-eared Owl co-exists with the closely related Long-eared Owl (*Asio otus*) but while both species hunt over open country and prey mostly on voles, the Long-eared Owl is strictly nocturnal, and the Short-ear takes over the habitat during the day.

All owls have a tremendous ability to rotate the head on the shoulders, as well as rolling it from side to side like a wheel. This ability is best developed in the Short-eared Owl which can pivot its head on its neck right over its back through an angle of 270 degrees, and also has great freedom of movement from side to side. Such movement is of great assistance in pinpointing the direction of a sound (as the head is moved the ears receive the sound from different angles) and is also important to the bird in that the eyes are totally immovable.

Short-eared Owls frequent open country and particularly favour marshy or boggy areas. They are territorial birds, maintaining a range of thirty or forty acres. They spend much of their time on the wing, hunting low over their territory; the flight is undulating with frequent periods of gliding. In display, during courtship flights, they occasionally fly much higher, and the male may clap his wings above his back. Short-eared Owls build a nest of grass on the ground in March or April, and lay from four to seven eggs. Incubation, by the female, begins with the first egg. Both territory size and clutchsize are to some extent regulated in relation to food supply. In addition, although the birds are usually single-brooded, a pair may produce and rear a second brood in response to an over-abundance of food.

Short-eared Owl

Plate 30. Little Owl (Athene noctua)

The Little Owl is readily recognised as a small owl, about eight inches high with a distinctively squat, flat-headed appearance. It is also unusual amongst the owls in that it is often seen in daylight. As in most owls, the back plumage is grey-brown, mottled and streaked with white, the underparts white, with darker streaks. Little Owls have no 'ear-tufts' and a very poorly-developed facial disc. The eyes, too, are small, as befits its largely diurnal habit, and the brows are low, as if the bird were permanently frowning in concentration. The tail is short, the wings broad and rounded – almost moth-like. Little Owls are widely distributed throughout Eurasia between 30°N and 50°N and are birds of fairly open country – mixed farmland, parkland or other relatively level ground broken by hedges or copses. They were introduced into Britain after a number of attempts, and were first recorded breeding in 1879 in Kent. Later they spread throughout England and Wales, although they do not yet occur in Scotland or Ireland.

Little Owls feed throughout the year on insects, chiefly earwigs, craneflies and large beetles such as cockchafers; they will also take mammals up to the size of large rats. Despite the suspicion on first introduction of the birds to Britain that they destroyed poultry and gamebird chicks, the intensive study by the British Trust for Ornithology of the prey of Little Owls which it prompted revealed that birds form a very small part of the diet indeed. The owls hunt both by day and night. They perch frequently on tree stumps or fenceposts, and, when alarmed or excited – for example, on first sighting possible prey – the bird bobs up and down on its perch. This behaviour is absolutely characteristic of Little Owls. The flight is silent, low, and deeply undulating – again a distinctive feature. Rather more terrestrial than most owls, they frequently settle on the ground and are able to run quite fast in pursuing prey.

The owls breed in holes in trees, walls or cliffs, in burrows in the ground and occasionally on the ground itself. The female incubates the clutch of between three and five eggs herself, fed by the male.

Both in appearance and general habits, Little Owls resemble the Burrowing Owl of North America (*Speotyto cunicularia*). This species has the same characteristic, undulating flight of the Little Owl, and the same habit of bobbing on a perch when alarmed. It, too, breeds in burrows on the ground or on the ground surface, and feeds on insects and small rodents. In the New World, it very much takes over the ecological role held by the Little Owl in Eurasia.

The Little Owl has long been surrounded by superstition and myth. It is portrayed as the Owl of Wisdom – the companion and familiar of the Greek goddess Pallas Athene, from whom it takes its scientific name. It was, and is, regarded by many as a bird of ill-omen; perhaps in some measure from its scowling countenance and shrill, eerie call.

A pair of Little Owls on a favourite perch.

Little Owl

Plate 31. Eagle Owl (Bubo bubo)

Eagle Owls are amongst the largest of the owls: majestic birds standing up to nearly thirty inches high and weighing perhaps eight or nine pounds. They occur throughout the world and might be considered the nocturnal equivalent of diurnal raptors such as eagles or buzzards. The largest of them all is the European Eagle Owl, a huge bird found all over Eurasia, from as far north as the Arctic Circle in Scandinavia, east across Russia, and south to Arabia, Iran, India and China.

In Europe, Eagle Owls are usually found in craggy, timber-clad areas; elsewhere in their range they occur in all types of habitat, from dense forest – coniferous or deciduous, to mountain or desert areas which may be completely treeless. With such a wide geographical distribution, and such a variety of habitats, the species is variable in form. All are huge owls, with heavy, compressed bills and enormous talons, with mottled, brown backs and lighter underparts, heavily streaked with dark brown; all have marked 'ear-tufts'. The plumage is darkest in forest areas, becoming sandier in arid and semi-desert regions. The owls reach their largest size, some twenty-eight inches high and with a wing span of five feet, in high latitudes, being somewhat smaller towards the south of their range. An obvious characteristic is the call, a deep booming "ooo-hu" – with emphasis on the first syllable.

Their huge size enables Eagle Owls to kill really quite sizeable prey. The largest kill ever recorded for a European Eagle Owl was of a roe deer weighing nearly thirty pounds (taken by an owl of little over eight pounds!). Despite this, Eagle Owls usually feed on smaller species, animals very little larger than those taken by other owl species, preying for the most part on small game birds and rodents: brown rats, voles, mice and lemmings. A study of the diet of Eagle Owls in Sweden showed that some fifty-five percent of the food was composed of small mammals, while birds made up a further thirty-three percent. Eagle Owls are a strongly territorial species, maintaining their territories throughout the year. Each breeding area holds several nest sites, which are usually used in alternation. (This seems, for some reason, to be a characteristic of all the larger birds of prey, for the eagles and many other large hawks also maintain many nests and use them in rotation. It is almost as if it is a habit adopted once the bird reaches a certain size limit.) The nest site is usually on a rocky outcrop or cliff-edge, and the nest is little more than a scrape in the ground. Occasionally, old nests of eagles or buzzards may be occupied. Three or four eggs are laid and the female starts to incubate after laying the second egg. The young thus hatch asynchronously, and the youngest ones usually die unless food is particularly abundant. The clutch is always completed surprisingly early, often while there is still snow on the ground. This is because the young owls grow very slowly and cannot fly properly for many weeks. Even after the owlets are flighted, it is many months before they become independent of their parents, for they take a long time to learn to hunt. (While all owls hunt instinctively, many have to learn how actually to kill their prey, and all need time to develop their hunting skills to a level where they become reasonably proficient at catching them.)

Closely related to the European Eagle Owl, and very similar in all respects, is the Great Horned Owl *(Bubo virginianus)* of America, found throughout the New World from the Arctic to the Straits of Magellan. Great Horned Owls are slightly smaller birds with, in consequence, a smaller maximum size of prey; there are also certain differences in plumage, in that the Great Horned Owl is somewhat greyer and has a stripier plumage than does the European Eagle Owl. Heavily barred below, it has a conspicuous white throat collar, and is the only *large* American owl to have ear-tufts. Characteristic of both woodland and open country, the Great Horned Owl is often considered the complementary species to the American Red-tailed Hawk *(Buteo jamaicensis)*. Each hunts similar prey over the same type of habitat, the one replacing the other as day turns to night.

Like European Eagle Owls, Great Horned Owls feed mainly on small rodents: rats, mice and rabbits, despite the potential variety of larger prey items they could take. In Canada, towards the Arctic regions, Great Horned Owls rely for their food to a very large extent on Varying Hares. This species shows a marked and regular periodicity in abundance over a ten-year cycle, and, in harmony with this change, the populations of the owls, too, fluctuate over a ten-year cycle. Similar cycles have been suggested in the numbers of European Eagle Owls in Russia, but are less clearly defined.

Eagle Owl

Plate 32. Snowy Owl (Nyctea scandiaca)

Female Snowy Owl alighting at nest beside young.

Closely related to the Eagle Owl (*Bubo bubo*) and occupying the equivalent ecological niche in the treeless tundras of the Arctic, is the Snowy Owl. A great white owl, only slightly smaller than the Eagle Owl, the Snowy Owl occurs north of the treeline right around the pole, breeding as far north as there is land that is not under permanent ice or snow. The colouring is very variable; some Snowies are pure white, others have varying amounts of dark streaking upon the feathers, even to the extent of having almost a blue-grey mantle and back. Although crepuscular by choice, hunting in the early morning and late evening, the short Arctic days and comparative scarcity of food forces them to fly through much of the day, so that they become almost diurnal.

As might be imagined from their chosen habitat, Snowy Owls are opportunistic hunters, feeding on a wide variety of prey, including ground squirrels, ducks and gamebirds, such as Arctic Ptarmigan. The most important prey species, however, are lemmings and Arctic Hares; the extent to which the Owls rely on these species is clearly shown in the way their population numbers fluctuate in step with the cycles of abundance of lemmings and hares. As a general ecological rule, the simpler a system, the less stable it is. Hence, in the simple ecological community that exists in the Arctic, it is not always easy for owls to keep their population size adjusted to that of their prey abundance. Every so often there is a sudden, 'unexpected' decline in prey when owl numbers are at their peak. As a result, the owls migrate in search of food, and are seen far to the south of their normal range – even reaching as far as southern Europe, India and the southern United States. Such irruptions belie, however, the essentially sedentary nature of the species, whose wintering range in normal years extends only a short distance to the south of its breeding range.

Snowy Owls breed on the ground, with the eggs laid in a simple scrape in the tundra. Like the Eagle Owl, they start to breed very early, for the young are dependent on the adults for a considerable period. Indeed, the problem is further compounded by the short Arctic summer; there is hardly enough time for the owlets to gain their full hunting skill before the rigours of winter. Clutch-size is variable, and highly dependent on prey abundance: between five and eight eggs is probably the normal number. Eggs tend to be laid every other day, but with the unpredictability of food they are sometimes laid at longer and much more irregular intervals. Incubation begins with the first egg, so that the brood eventually consists of young often of markedly different ages. As usual, the youngest die if there is insufficient food to go round, ensuring that the brood is quickly adjusted to the maximum size for the available resources. But in fact, very few of the young survive anyway. Despite the size and solicitousness of the parent owls, there are heavy losses to predators – Arctic Foxes and Skuas – and there is a further heavy mortality when the young attain independence, for many have simply not had time to develop their hunting skills to a sufficient pitch to face the scarcity of prey over winter.

Snowy Owls have recently become established as a regularly breeding species in Britain. The first pair bred on Fetlar in the Shetland Islands in 1967 – the rocky island with its short turf and bare outcrops proving an ideal habitat. The nest was closely guarded by volunteer wardens of the Royal Society for the Protection of Birds; their vigil has been maintained ever since, and the Snowies return to Fetlar year after year.

Snowy Owl

Plate 33. Scops Owl (Otus scops)

The group of owls to which the Scops Owl belongs are small, nocturnal owls, most of them found in tropical or subtropical regions of the world. Only a few live in more temperate areas, amongst them the Screech Owls of North America (*Otus asio* and *O. kennicotti*) and the Scops Owls (*Otus scops* and *O. sunia*) of Europe and Asia.

The European Scops Owl (*Otus scops*) ranges from North Africa through Europe and much of Asia. In the northern part of its range it is migratory, moving south to spend the winter on the African savannahs. Throughout their range, Scops Owls favour open country with isolated trees, or clusters of trees; in the north they also inhabit birch and conifer forests. They prey largely on insects, but will also take lizards and small mammals.

The Scops Owl is one of the smallest of all the owls, being only some seven and a half inches high. It has a closely striped plumage of grey and brown, streaked with white on the back and dark brown below; it has small 'ear-tufts', often barely noticeable, and the facial disc is less pronounced than in other owls. The plumage is highly cryptic; when the bird roosts by day on the side branch of a tree, standing tall, and pressed close to the trunk, it is beautifully camouflaged, blending right into the trunk itself, the streaks and speckles of its plumage looking just like bark lines or patches of lichen. Most characteristic is the call, a monotonous piping repeated every couple of seconds or so. Each whistle, apparently single, is in fact made up of a rapid tremolo. The call has often been mistaken for that of the Midwife Toad. This call is most common during the breeding season.

Soon after they have returned from their winter quarters, the males take up territories, and sing near the chosen nest site to attract a female. This nest site is usually a hole in a tree (particularly old woodpecker holes) or in a ruined building, though almost any high crevice may be used. Once the male has found a mate, the pair may then sing in duet. The female occupies the nest site shortly before laying the first egg. From this time she never leaves it but stays in the nest hole throughout the day. She usually lays a clutch of four or five eggs. A German scientist has noted with his tame Scops Owls that the female remained in the nest crevice until she had laid the penultimate egg. During this period, the male brings food to his mate and passes it in through the nest entrance. He also brings food while the female is incubating and provides for the brood once they have hatched. Often, he may collect up quite a supply of food and store it near the nest site in crevices and niches until needed. This caching habit is thought to be unique amongst owls.

This photograph clearly demonstrates the effective camouflage in the plumage of the Scops Owl.

Scops Owl

Plate 34. Boreal Owl
(Aegolius funereus)

The Boreal, Tengmalm's, Owl by John Gould.

The Boreal Owl is a small owl, measuring about ten inches in height, very reminiscent in appearance of a scaled-down version of the Tawny Owl *(Strix aluco)*. It has the same freckled plumage, large head and well-defined facial disc; the head is, however, less rounded, and the facial disc is split by a pronounced 'widow's peak', where the white spotted crown projects down over the brow. The eyes are yellow (while those of the Tawny Owl are large and glossy black) and the legs and feet are completely covered in white feathers. The call is very distinctive, a soft flute-like note repeated at intervals of a few seconds, "poo-poo-poo", usually with variations in stress. It has been likened to the regular dropping of water.

The Boreal Owl, or Richardson's Owl, has a wide distribution in both Europe (where it is known as Tengmalm's Owl) and North America. It is chiefly a bird of northern coniferous forests, especially amongst spruce or pine in Scandinavia across through northern Russia in the Old World, and in North America. However, in pine forests on high ground, there are also populations further south towards Central America and central Europe, and locally, the birds may inhabit more mixed woodland, with birch and poplar. This owl is a sedentary and non-migratory species.

During the continuous light of the far northern summer, the owl of course must feed during the day, but elsewhere it is chiefly nocturnal, spending the daylight hours in a hole in a tree, or in the tops of the conifers. It preys upon small birds and mammals usually taken from a perch. Boreal Owls nest in tree-holes – often the disused nest-hole of a woodpecker. For some reason as yet undiscovered, clutches are significantly smaller in North America – three to six eggs as against up to ten in Europe. The four-week incubation starts with the first egg, and thus, as in most birds of prey, there is an asynchronous hatching of the chicks, the youngest usually dying except in years of exceptional prey abundance.

Boreal Owl

Plate 35. Hawk Owl (Surnia ulula)

The Hawk Owl is a bird of northern coniferous forests around the whole of the northern hemisphere. Within this area it is found in open spaces, in clearings, in open parts of the forest where the trees are widely spaced, or where the woodland is broken with patches of deciduous trees. It is also found in scrub or in thinly scattered trees on the edge of the tundra. They are markedly diurnal birds, rather shrike-like in appearance and behaviour, generally perching on a high vantage point, and swooping down on prey from this look-out.

Hawk Owls have long wings which taper to a point, and a long, rounded tail: a combination which gives swift, direct flight, and confers upon the bird the appearance of a hawk or small falcon, rather than that of an owl. They are medium-seized owls – about the same size as Long-eared Owls (*Asio otus*): a low brow splits the small facial disc into two distinct parts. The plumage is boldly marked: the crown is closely chequered like fine gingham cloth in black and white, the rest of the back mottled and barred in dark-brown and grey. The wings and tail are boldly barred in black and white. The underparts are white, covered with close transverse bars of black, and the grey facial disc is black-rimmed. The diurnal habits of this owl are reflected in additional features: the yellow eyes are small, and the ears lack the specialised asymmetry so necessary for location of sound in night owls.

The hunting method, as has been suggested, is rather shrike-like, the owl using a high vantage point to watch for prey and then swooping down onto its victim. It flies fast and low – the hawk-like outlines giving rapid manoeuvrable flight – swooping up to land at a new look-out. Occasionally, an owl may be seen to hunt from the air, flying higher and more slowly, and dropping onto its prey from a brief hover. The main prey are rodents, small mice, voles and lemmings, but it will also take larger mammals such as squirrels, where available, and a variety of small birds. As with all the boreal predators we have described here, the food supply is affected strongly by cycles of rodent abundance, and, as with these other species, clutchsize and breeding success fluctuate in harmony with the variations in numbers of their principal prey species. In really bad years, too, Hawk Owls move southwards in large numbers at the beginning of winter, appearing in areas well to the south of their normal range in irruptions typical of the other Arctic species, Snowy Owls (*Nyctea scandiaca*) and Rough-legged Buzzards (*Buteo lagopus*).

Clutchsize, varying with food supply, may be as low as three or four eggs in poor years, as high as ten or twelve in good years. The eggs are laid in a natural hole or cavity in trees, a typical nest site being provided by the hollow within the broken tip of a tall tree stump, or a large woodpecker hole. The nest is usually unlined. Hawk Owls are quite strongly territorial, and the soft musical hoot is used as a territorial call. A sharp chattering whistle, "ki-ki-ki-ki-ki", again more like that of a hawk than an owl, is also heard at the beginning of the breeding season.

Hawk Owl

Acknowledgements

Photographs were kindly supplied by the following:
Aquila Photographics: *R. J. C. Blewitt* 31; *Dennis Green* 62, 70,
86, 108; *W. S. Paton* 28/29; *Donald Platt* 60; *Donald A. Smith*
84, 98/99; *E. K. Thompson* 17; *M. C. Wilkes* 30, 56, 90. Ardea
London: *Uno Berggren* 38/39; *R. J. C. Blewitt* 72; *Ake Lindau* 13;
P. Morris 58; *Alan Weaving* 114. Christopher Dawes: 40/41.
Frank W. Lane: *G. Ronald Austing* 66; *Lynwood M. Chace* 68;
Georg Nystrand 42/43, 54. Royal Society for the Protection of
Birds: *Ian Fraser* 88; *Arthur Gilpin* 84; *P. van Groenendael* and
W. Suetens 12, 80, 104; *Eric Hosking* 21, 26/27, 112; *Fritz
Pölking* 86, *Bobby Tulloch* 22.

The publishers are grateful to the following artists for permission
to reproduce their work: to J. C. Harrison for his drawings of
Golden Eagles on pages 23 and 60; to Eric Ennion for his wash
drawing of a Honey Buzzard on page 52 and the Marsh Harrier
on page 80; to Donald Watson for his study of the food pass of
the Hen Harrier/Marsh Hawk on page 76.

Special line drawings on pages 10, 11, 14/15, 16 and 106 are by
Paddy Sellars and distribution maps by Michael Robinson.